THE ISLE OF MAN
COASTAL PATH

Spectacular cliff scenery at The Chasms, overlooking the Sugarloaf

THE ISLE OF MAN COASTAL PATH

'Raad ny Foillan'
THE WAY OF THE GULL

Includes also the Millennium Way and
the 'Bayr ny Skeddan', The Herring Way

Aileen Evans

CICERONE PRESS
MILNTHORPE, CUMBRIA

Acknowledgements

I should like to thank the many people who have helped me along the way and with the writing of this guide. Sylvia Nuttall for her companionship and encouragement which was not dampened by the rain. Albert Riding for being my 'minder' and providing photographs. John and Bernie Craig of Spinning Wheel Antiques for their help and hospitality; W.S.Basnett, Jerry Jones, Robin Hynes, John Llewellyn and Margaret Quirk for much useful information. For photographs, the maps and drawings I must thank my husband Brian who patiently packed up at a moment's notice to follow me round the island.

Contents

*The site of the first Tynwald described in the Manx Sagas,
at Cronk Keeill Abban, close to the Millennium Way,
(see page 121).*

PREFACE

Raad ny Foillan - The Way of the Gull

The Raad ny Foillan (The Way of the Gull) is a 96 mile footpath around the coastline of the Isle of Man. This long-distance footpath was set up in 1986 to mark the island's Heritage Year. In its journey round the Isle of Man the Raad ny Foillan offers a variety of scenery from the rugged cliffs and mountain moorland in the south, to the glens, beaches and dunes of the north. It wends its way through two nature reserves and along an old disused railway. It passes scenes of historical interest, colourful fishing villages, and peaceful havens. It takes to the road in several places yet the country lanes have their own charm and little traffic. The single stretch of main road is of short duration. The footpath is never far from the sea or the cry of the gull. It is suitable for the gentle walker to do in short sections, for the back-packer to take his tent and leave the bustle of the city behind, and for the fit fellrunner to set up his own personal record for the delightful circuit of this beautiful island.

In this guide I have tried to introduce you to the Isle of Man as I have found it. As a child I visited Douglas and returned with memories of seaside bustle, horse-drawn trams and a lurching ship. My next visit was as a rock climber which fixed memories of a rugged, beautiful coastline and crags untouched by human hand. A third visit was as a backpacker to walk the coastal path. It far exceeded my expectations. After the first day, gone were all my pre-conceived ideas of a million motorbikes sporting kiss-me-quick stickers. I came away with pictures of dew on the primroses at Glen Maye, the sunset turning the surf to mobile gold and the wet noses of the seals as they questioned my presence so close to their domain. I hope that as you follow the Manx footpaths you will collect as many happy memories as I did.

The Introduction covers the practicalities necessary to organise the 'expedition', interesting things to be seen on the way and their back-ground.

The description of the footpath sets out the circuit in stages, the longest being 15½ miles, the shortest 7 miles. The fast walker may wish to complete two stages per day, those progressing at a more sedate pace may decide to amble along and take in the diverting attractions along the way. I chose to begin at Douglas simply because I arrived by boat and was keen to literally step from the quay onto the footpath. As the way borders Ronaldsway airport the starting point is a matter of choice and presents no problem.

The footpath is waymarked and together with the information given in the guide should enable the walker to progress easily and, if adverse conditions arise, safely.

The idea of a coastal footpath was first promoted by a former Governor of the Island, Sir Ambrose Flux Dunas, himself a keen rambler. There was no legislation similar to the Parks and Countryside Act in the U.K. but he paved the way for the 1961 Rights of Way Act. By 1973 maps were prepared and the task of waymarking and improving sections of the coastal path began. Mr Dave Wood, the Rights of Way Officer, was the man who took on the task and in the Heritage Year, 1986, the Raad ny Foillan was opened.

You will have realised by now that, although the Isle of Man sits snuggly in the Irish Sea surrounded by the British Isles, it is different from the rest of the United Kingdom. Though the Isle of Man is part of the mainland telephone network, the money you put in the slot is likely to be Manx: the Manx government issue their own currency which is legal tender only on the Island. They issue their own stamps also and if you post anything on the island, it must have a Manx stamp.

The pace of life is easy; people seem to have time to talk. I had an entertaining chat with a group of school children over the playground wall. I obtained some helpful advice from a gang of Commissioners, (we would call them council workers) who were laying a hedge. A fisherman mending his nets was only too pleased to inform me of the state of the Irish Sea and its fish over the last ten years. (Things are improving by the way.)

Although the early Manxmen were of Celtic origin, Man was part of the Norwegian Kingdom of the Hebrides until 1266. It is now a Self-Governing Crown Dependency, the Lieutenant-Governor being the Queen's representative on the Island.

The legislature, called The Tynwald, has two branches. The first is The Legislative Council which comprises The Bishop, The Attorney and eight members. The other branch is The House of Keys which has twenty-four elected members. The Isle of Man has a special relationship with the European Community but does not contribute to, nor receive, funds from the E.E.C. budget.

Douglas is the capital of the island, a position held by Castletown until 1869. It is the home of Manx Radio which was the first commercial radio station in the British Isles.

An important difference which affects the Raad ny Foillan is that caravans are not allowed on the Island and so it remains free from the coastal developments which have so despoiled much of Britain's coastline. The Manx treat their coastline as a prized asset and are making every effort to maintain its present beauty. Long-distance walkers will inevitably compare the Raad ny Foillan favourably with the South West Peninsula Path of Devon and Cornwall, where huge caravan sites often dominate the scenery.

Important to the thirsty walker, the licensing laws are different too. Pubs are open all day Monday to Saturday where you can sample the real Manx ale. An ancient law prohibits the use of any substitutes for malt, sugar or hops, so you do get the real stuff. The Manx ice-cream is the real stuff too and has received the accolade of the highest award in Britain. I cannot vouch for the ale, but I can definitely give the thumbs up to the ice-cream.

Aileen Evans
Preston 1987

9

INTRODUCTION

How to get there

The Isle of Man Steam Packet Company have regular sailings to Douglas from Heysham and Liverpool. Boat trains provide an economical way to travel as the Rail-Boat package is at a reduced fare. Car parking is available at the dock.

Excursion boats sail from Fleetwood; June to September on Tuesdays and some Wednesdays and can be used for a single journey. Tel: (039) 17 79573.

Belfast and Dublin sailings are from May to September.

Fare reductions for groups are available.

Details of timetables and fares are available in the Isle of Man Steam Packet Seaways brochure, available from all travel agents, British Rail enquiry offices or -

> Isle of Man Steam Packet Seaways,
> Imperial Buildings,
> Douglas, Isle of Man. Tel: (0624) 661661

> Isle of Man Steam Packet Seaways, Sea Terminal,
> Heysham, Lancs, LA3 2XF Tel: (0524) 53802

All boats are drive on/off car ferries. Bicycles are transported free. To me the chief delight is that dogs are allowed and moreover go free, so I had the pleasure of the company of my four footed friend, a sad loss on my foreign backpacks. The overnight boat from Heysham arrives in time for you to enjoy the dawn from the footpath - a worthwhile bonus.

If you plan to travel by air there is a daily service to Ronaldsway from the following airports: Belfast City, Birmingham, Blackpool, Cardiff, Dublin, Glasgow, Liverpool, London Heathrow, Luton, Manchester.

In the summer (May-Sept. but check the dates at your travel agent as they vary slightly each year), Saturday only flights are available at budget fares. The condition attached to the budget fare is that you spend one Saturday night on the Island and return within a month. These Saturday flights are tailor-made to do the coastal footpath as you can begin within a mile of the airport gateway.

Luggage is limited to 15kgs and one piece of hand luggage.

Manx Airlines Limited,
Isle of Man (Ronaldsway) Airport,
Ballasalla.
Central Reservations - Open 6.30am-20.00 daily.
Tel: (0624) 824111
Prestel: 461114
Fax: (0624) 824578
Current flight information Tel: (0624) 600600

The Best Time for the Walk

Everyone hopes for good weather and to some extent we can control this by looking at the past meteorological reports. During 1985 and 1986 May and June stood out as the months with a good sunshine average and little rainfall - unfortunately this is also the time of the T.T. Races (see below). The holiday season begins in June and is virtually over by mid-September yet in the middle of the season I met very few people on the footpath, except around the Sound Café where tourists were taking the air within sight of the car park. Most walkers that I met were Manx and were pleased to see a 'foreigner' enjoying their coastline. Spring brings the fresh leaves and flowers to the glens and migrant birds to the beaches. Late summer glows with the dwarf gorse in flower, heather in bloom and those indescribable sunsets from the west coast which make the stumbling about in the twilight to reach your destination worthwhile.

If there is a time of year to avoid it is late May, early June and early September; the weeks of the motorcycle and car rallies. At these times the ferries are fully booked and so is the accommodation. Camp sites are likely to be full and you will have little chance of procuring a prime spot when you arrive after a day's walk.

Having said all this, I walked the Millennium Way in the first weekend of the T.T. Practices. I met one other walker, a small group of scouts cooking baked beans and bacon over a wood fire, and a horse and rider. I camped in delectable surroundings and the weather was superb.

A provisional list of events for the year is published by the Isle of Man Tourist Board and is at the back of their classified list of accommodation.

Accommodation

The Manx Tourist Board, 13 Victoria Street, Douglas. Tel: (0624) 674323, Prestel 251218, Fax: (0624) 672872, issues a useful Directory of Accommodation and has a comprehensive information service. Of most interest to walkers is the Bed & Breakfast accommodation, available in many of the farms, towns and villages en route. However, the northern part of the island is sparsely served. The accommodation list preceding each section has been updated prior to printing, but changes can occur. It is advisable to check with the Tourist Board for the latest information.

For backpackers there is good news. Camping is allowed on common ground and anywhere else with permission of the landowner. There are camp sites with full facilities at Douglas, Peel and Glen Wyllin. Also a grassy spot by the beach at Glen Mooar. Farmers often allow camping and I have always found them most helpful. If you are prepared to carry your water, secluded places to pitch your tent abound, but remember, take your rubbish away with you and leave your site clean for others to enjoy.

(**NOTE** that the campsite at Castletown, marked on the I.O.M. Public Rights of Way and Outdoor Leisure Map and the Ordnance Survey Landranger Sheet 95 is not available for campers.)

Public Transport

The Isle of Man is well served with public transport, especially when the schools are in session. Buses, an electric railway and a steam railway cover the Island and the fares are modest.

The Isle of Man Passenger Transport Board publishes a booklet of official timetables which is available from any bus station, Tourist Information Office, or the Information Bureau at the Douglas Sea Terminal, for a few pence.

The steam train runs from Douglas, (Bank Hill Station is at the southern end of the harbour) to Port Erin. The whole line is within easy reach to the Raad ny Foillan. Stations along the line are: - Port Soderick, Santon, Ballasalla, Castletown, Ballabeg, Colby, Port St. Mary, Port Erin.

Open Easter, May-September daily.

The electric railway runs from Douglas, (Derby Castle Terminus is at the northern end of the promenade) to Laxey and Ramsey. There are numerous request halts along the way, the main ones being Groudle, Garwick, Dhoon, Ballaglass, Ballajora. The electric

railway runs from May-September daily.

From Laxey Station the Snaefell Mountain Railway makes the journey to the summit.

The bus service is more frequent in summer, May-September, when thirty routes criss-cross the Island. All the towns and large villages are on a bus route and special services run in the summer to Cregneish and the Sound from Port Erin. These services are too numerous and complicated to try to list here but of special interest to the walker is that the Douglas-Castletown-Port Erin, and the Peel-Castletown-Port Erin buses call at the Airport.

There is another form of public transport which you may find irresistible if you have blisters on the last lap, - the horsedrawn trams clip-clopping their way along Douglas promenade!

Climate

The climate of the Isle of Man can be summed up as being milder than that of its neighbours. The influence of the surrounding relatively warm sea is the major factor. In winter the temperatures seldom fall below freezing. The 42° isotherm, after passing through the Isle of Wight, swings northward to capture the Isle of Man. In summer the sea exerts a cooling influence and the Island enjoys the pleasant gap between the 58° and 60° isotherms. The annual amount of rainfall on the coastline is 30-40ins. per year, most of this falling in the winter months. As can be expected, it is heavier on the mountains. The wind often blows the clouds over the coastline leaving it dry whilst inland the hills are swathed in cloud. The prevailing wind is south-west. This is a consideration in planning your route. If you tackle the walk clockwise the length of the west coast will put any breeze at your back, then as you turn the Point of Ayre to come south the cliffs and mountains will provide shelter.

The following chart of the monthly rainfall and average daily hours of sunshine over the past year proves very interesting.

13

Dawn over the Tower of Refuge, Douglas Bay

		Sunshine and Rainfall Record. Douglas 1985-1986 S = Hours of sunshine. Av. daily R = Rainfall in mm.				
	July	**August**	**September**	**October**	**November**	**December**
S	4.6	4.1	3.1	2.8	2.2	1.7
R	126mm	196mm	115mm	57mm	174mm	146mm
	January	**February**	**March**	**April**	**May**	**June**
S	1.5	2.9	4.5	5.7	6.9	6.9
R	125mm	2mm	118mm	97mm	96mm	56mm

Another facet of the weather is the sea mist. The air over the sea can be saturated with water vapour. A drop of only one degree in temperature can result in the condensation of suspended vapour causing mist in the surrounding air. Thus mist can roll in from the sea with little warning and can be disorientating.

The Isle of Man has three excellent bonuses to offer weatherwise. To experience the unpolluted air of the Island (the 500 varieties of lichens will testify to its purity); to watch the opalescent dawn spread over the water and breathe its tints into the surf; to see the sun set behind the Mountains of Mourne. A poet is needed to describe this.

Tides and Times

The sea makes such a major contribution to the Raad ny Foillan that it is to our advantage to learn a little about its ways. Things that seem obvious and familiar to those fortunate enough to live near the sea, may be amusing, but could soon become alarming to those who make the odd visit to the sea and are not familiar with its various moods.

The tide flows up the Irish Sea in a northerly direction, bending round the Point of Ayre to take an easterly direction along the Galloway coast. The ebb flows at $2\frac{1}{2}$ knots from Galloway south back down the Irish Sea.

The tidal flow reaches Liverpool at roughly the same time as the Isle of Man, the tidal differences in time and height on Liverpool being:

(Reed's Nautical Almanac 1987)

	Mean High Water		Mean Low Water	
	Time Diff. H. Min	Ht. Diff Metres	Time Diff. H. Min	Ht. Diff. Metres
Ramsey	+0.05	-1.8	-0.05	-0.3
Laxey	0.00	-2.0	-0.15	-0.3
Peel	0.00	-3.6	-0.05	-0.9

The times and heights of the tides for Liverpool can be found easily in the national daily newspapers, Reed's Nautical Almanac or Brown's Nautical Almanac.

The tidal stream changes direction every six hours. The ebb usually runs longer than six hours whilst the flood runs slightly less than six hours, low tide being 6hrs.10mins. after high tide. This results in advancing the time of high water and low water by three quarters of an hour every twenty four hours.

The strength of the tidal stream varies daily because of the position of the moon. The tide height and range is greatest at Spring tides. Spring tides occur 2 days after New and Full moons, Neap tides fortnightly halfway between Spring tides, 2 days after the First and Last quarters of the moon. Spring tide height at Liverpool is considered high at 9 metres but twice a year makes 10 metres. This is a result of the influence of the sun and the moon, and occurs at the Vernal Equinox (21st March) and the Autumnal Equinox (21st September).

INTRODUCTION

Another feature of interest to us on the Raad ny Foillan is the influence the wind has on the height of the waves. I had heard of freak waves arriving from nowhere but had never fully appreciated the extra wave height generated by a modest breeze. The following chart will help you gauge the height of the waves on the sea and the extra amount of water they may throw at you above the normal high tide. I cannot resist the fascination of waves dashing over the rocks and exploding against the cliffs. A real bonus to be enjoyed in bad weather - from a safe distance of course.

BEAUFORT WIND SCALE				
m.p.h.			**Ht of waves**	**appearance**
0	less than 1	calm	-	mirror
1	1-3	light	0.1 metres	ripples
2	4-6	light breeze	0.2 metres	small wavelets
3	7-10	gen. breeze	0.6 metres	large wavelets
4	11-16	mod. breeze	1 metre	small waves
5	17-21	fresh breeze	2 metres	mod. waves,horses
6	22-27	strong breeze	3 metres	large waves, many horses,spray
7	27-34	near gale	4 metres	sea heaps
8	34-40	gale	5.5 metres	mod. high waves

Maps and Compasses

The maps in this guide are sufficient to enable you to walk the Raad ny Foillan but you will need to step off it from time to time. A map of the Island will help you to obtain the maximum enjoyment, replenish your supplies and be sure of your nearest point of help in the case of an emergency. Along with the map you will need a compass and know how to use it.

The Isle of Man Public Rights of Way and Leisure Map marks the Raad ny Foillan (The Way of the Gull) and the two shorter footpaths, The Millennium Way and the Bayr ny Skeddan (The Herring Way). The scale is 1:25,000 (2½ inches to the mile or 4cm to 1km) and it is a wonderful map for detail. It is a map that you can enjoy in your armchair. The key will indicate the meaning of the various symbols shown on the map. Almost every cove and headland is named, every field drawn. The contour lines, imaginary lines passing through all places of equal height, are at 100ft intervals. By roughly orientating the map you will be able to identify the mountains and surrounding countryside. (The top of the map is north. Place your compass on one of the vertical grid lines on your map and rotate the map until the grid line is parallel with the compass needle.) This method is approximate and is not good enough if you are assailed by a thick mist. In this case:

1. Place your compass on the map with the rotating capsule turned so that the north arrow on the dial is in its correct position at 0 (or 360°), and with the whole compass pointing north to the top of the map. The grid lines will help you to do this.

2. Slowly rotate the map keeping the compass firmly in place, still pointing to the top of the map (north), until the compass needle swings and points to the magnetic north which is 5° west of true north (1986) or 355°. your map is now set and you should be able to follow the desired direction.

The Isle Of Man Public Rights of Way and Leisure Map is one large sheet printed on both sides which makes it rather unwieldy, but your rapid progress along its folds really boosts the ego. One feature of this map which may cause difficulty is the tiny printing of the names. If you want to delve into every detail you may need a magnifying glass. The Ordnance Survey map of the Isle of Man - Landranger 1:50,000 Sheet No. 95 is a revised issue 1987, but the marking of the three long distance footpaths lacks detail.

Before you set out it will be useful if you send for the tourist literature supplied liberally by the Isle of Man Tourist Board. In the brochures there are street maps of the towns. I cut out these maps and stuck them in a small notebook together with the boat, bus and rail timetables. I found these little street maps most helpful and time saving, especially at the end of the day.

Geology

If you have no interest in geology when you begin the Raad ny Foillan you are sure to have your interest aroused in the first few miles. If you have a general basic knowledge you will be excited by the strata on view. If you are a geologist you will be continually left behind and will have to restrain yourself from getting out your lump hammer and loading yourself and your companions with samples! As you progress from Douglas clockwise round the Island

Contorted rock folds at The Whing

you will be introduced to rocks from very old to the most recent at the Point of Ayre, then as you move down the east coast you will be able to recognise them again as old friends.

The Isle of Man has few crags inland, but the stone used in the old local walls and buildings, and the vegetation cover will give you clues to the nature of the underlying rocks. At the coast however, the rock strata is exposed, washed and ready for inspection.

The Isle of Man is part of the Irish Sea horst. In layman's terms a horst is a ridge pushed up between two great faults, cracks in the earth. In Cambro-Ordovician times layers of muds and silts known as the Manx or Barrule Slates were deposited. Movements in the earth's crust caused subsidence which was followed by marine deposition when the carboniferous limestones were deposited. Next came a period of uplift and folding. This movement produced the Irish Sea horst, the plateau-like area. This horst extends from Ireland to the English Lake District, the Isle of Man being the central part protruding above the waters of the Irish Sea. The folded Barrule Slates can be seen from the Marine Drive where they give rise to magnificent coastal scenery. In the Tertiary period dykes, vertical cracks filled from below with molten basalt, occurred in profusion, cutting through the strata resulting in sudden changes of colour and texture.

18

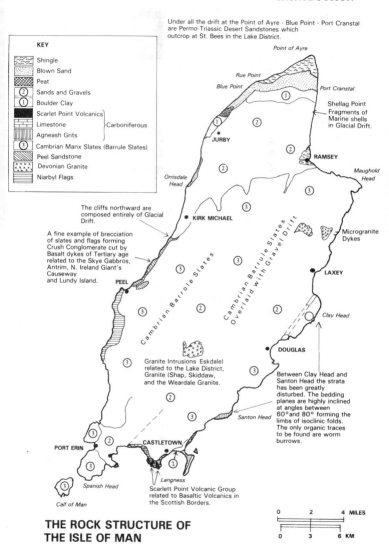

Under all the drift at the Point of Ayre - Blue Point - Port Cranstal are Permo-Triassic Desert Sandstones which outcrop at St. Bees in the Lake District.

KEY

- Shingle
- Blown Sand
- Peat
- ② Sands and Gravels
- ① Boulder Clay
- Scarlet Point Volcanics
- Limestone ⎱ Carboniferous
- Agneash Grits ⎰
- ③ Cambrian Manx Slates (Barrule Slates)
- Peel Sandstone
- Devonian Granite
- Niarbyl Flags

Shellag Point
Fragments of Marine shells in Glacial Drift.

Maughold Head

The cliffs northward are composed entirely of Glacial Drift.

A fine example of brecciation of slates and flags forming Crush Conglomerate cut by Basalt dykes of Tertiary age related to the Skye Gabbros, Antrim, N. Ireland Giant's Causeway and Lundy Island.

Microgranite Dykes

Cambrian Barrule Slates

Cambrian Barrule Slates Overlaid with Gravel Drift

Clay Head

Granite Intrusions Eskdale) related to the Lake District, Granite (Shap, Skiddaw, and the Weardale Granite.

Between Clay Head and Santon Head the strata has been greatly disturbed. The bedding planes are highly inclined at angles between 60° and 80° forming the limbs of isoclinic folds. The only organic traces to be found are worm burrows.

Santon Head

Langness

Scarlett Point Volcanic Group related to Basaltic Volcanics in the Scottish Borders.

Spanish Head

Calf of Man

THE ROCK STRUCTURE OF THE ISLE OF MAN

| 0 | 2 | 4 MILES |
| 0 | 3 | 6 KM |

INTRODUCTION

During the ice ages glaciers covered the Island. As they moved south they carried with them large boulders from Scotland which were subsequently deposited as erratics. Many of these have been used in buildings. As the glaciers crossed the sea they scooped up and carried marine deposits from the sea bed. As the ice melted sands, gravels and boulder clays were abandoned. During its passage the ice planed away some areas of the Manx slates to expose the underlying granite.

In recent geological times raised beaches were formed in the north of the Island. Accumulations of peat and blown sand are still in the process of settling, completing the geological picture of the Island for you to examine at close quarters from the footpath.

The visible geological strata to be seen are:

Recent	*Blown Sand:* The Ayres, Jurby, Andreas, Poyllvaaishi, Langness
	Peat: In beds; on the hills and mountains
	Alluvium and river drift: Southern plain
	Marine Raised Beach: Derby Haven, Cass-ny-Hawin
Glacial	*Sand and gravels:* The Bride hills and scattered mounds
	Boulder clay and rubble drift: Blue Point, south of Port Cranstal
Carboniferous	*Limestone series:* Castletown, Scarlett
	Basement Sandstone: Peel
	Basement Conglomerate: Langness, Ballasalla, Peel
Upper Cambrian	*Manx Slates. (Barrule Slates, Agneash Grits, Crush Conglomerates, Lonan and Niarbyl Flags)* See map p.19 for locations.
Igneous Rocks	*Granite:* Santon, Foxdale, Dhoon

Nature Along the Footpaths

One of the delights of the Raad ny Foillan is the contrast of the vast expanse of sea and sky with the intimate environment of the plants at your feet and birds skimming over your head.

The mild, damp climate is without extremes of temperature, but the continually changing base rocks and the soil they support must be the main factor contributing to the variety of plant and animal life we are likely to see on the way.

PLANTS

In the book *The Flowering Plants of the Isle of Man* we are told that there are 38 varieties of fern and fern allies, 853 flowering plants and 9 types of conifer to be found on the Island. Some are very rare and best left to prosper in their secret havens. Others show off their flowers, generously lining the footpath and a limited description of what to expect and where, will perhaps be helpful.

The mountains and headlands are mainly of Barrule Slate. The highest mountain is Snaefell (2,036ft.) and is rather low for mountain species although a few can be seen. The peaty soil supports a mixture of gorse and heather. The common gorse was introduced for fodder, fuel, and reinforcing the banked hedgerows. The dwarf gorse which flowers in the late summer is native to the Island. Bracken and cotton grass take no finding but the tiny asphodel, white and yellow bedstraw, sundew and the violet and vetches which seems to grow everywhere need a little more careful attention if you are to enjoy them.

The glens, sheltered from the winds, are veritable greenhouses and the common trees and plants which grow there appear more vibrant than normal. The stems are taller, the colours brighter, scents unrecognised hang in the air, ferns and mosses take on an artistic grace previously unnoticed. Palm trees and fuchia grow with the abandoned air of a native plant and it is often difficult to know where the cultivation ends and nature takes over. The lanes encountered are often between high stone and sod walls. Overgrown during the years since their youth, the stones are often hidden by a cascade of flowers best seen in the spring. Bluebells, celandine, primroses, yellow poppies and violets intermingled with buds of promise belonging to ramsons, red campion, and greater stitchwort with the wild rose and sweet briar patiently waiting for the summer. Where the stone is on view, ground ivy, stonecrop and pennywort do their best to clothe it with the rue-leaved saxifrage and herb robert adding their own distinctive colours.

The limestone of Scarlett Point has its own nature trail and Visitor Centre. A small, yet comprehensive booklet is available. Flowers of the limestone and those loving the proximity of the sea abound. Sea thrift, white sea campion, buttercup and bird's foot

Sand spurrey at Scarlett Point

trefoil cannot be missed, but just through the gate by the coast-guard station on the path, the minute mauve and white flowers of the sand spurrey and the purple thyme, can be easily overlooked. The spring squill abounds amongst the short turf and on the basalt dykes lichens can be examined. The lichen is a dual plant, a fungus determining the shape, living with an alga, its chlorophyll making the food. The two varieties on the basalt are as different as chalk and cheese. *Romalina Siliquosa* is the 'tall' grey spiky one, *Lecanora Atra* is the flat, frill-like, orange one. Two of the five hundred varieties on the Island.

The sand and gravels of the north are still blowing about and settling according to the whim of the weather. This is an area of unique scientific interest and as you would expect, its welfare is guarded by the Ayres Nature Reserve. Marram grass is the first plant to stabilize the sand with its network of strong roots forming a rampart along the dunes. Behind its protection, sea holly, pink-flowered sea bindweed and the green-flowered sea spurge are found. A little further inland where there is a sandy soil, hawkweeds, brambles and restharrow grow. Where the sand is captured in the fixed dunes, burnet rose, orchids, ferns and lichens thrive, together with the Manx cabbage. The Manx cabbage, *Brassica Monensis,* was first discovered by the botanist John Ray in 1662. It has a tall stem topped by a crown of yellow flowers which turn to spreading seed pods as the summer progresses. Rare flowers flourish amongst the sand dunes, uncommon orchids, lichens and ferns. Do not disturb them or gather their seeds. Some orchids do not produce seeds until about 14 years old. How tragic to trample on one that was thirteen and a half!

For a while the footpath uses a man-made fabrication - a railway track, now closed and abandoned. But not for long. New tenants have arrived, in the form of lady's smock, red campion and various grasses. Now these new tenants have visitors, the meadow brown, wall brown, and the orange tip butterflies. The bird's foot tre-foil is host to the common blue, the small copper likes to stay with the dock or sorrel, while the tall stinging nettles stand like hotels for the peacock, tor-toiseshell and red admiral. Other butterflies such as the large, small, and grey-veined whites have moved in, so you are likely to see many caterpil-lars about. You are the passing visitor here so take care not to tread on them.

The Isle of Man Cabbage
Brassica Monensis

BIRDS

The Island has its share of resident birds but its position, roughly in the centre of the Irish Sea, makes it an important staging post for many migrants. Binoculars are a heavy addition to the rucksack if you are backpacking, but the long-distance footpaths give a grandstand view, and the birds are so little disturbed that they almost ignore you and make the binoculars redundant. An excel-lent comprehensive book *Birds of the Isle of Man,* by J.P.Cullen & P.P.Jennings and beautifully illustrated by Alan Harris, will tell you every detail of the Manx birdlife, so I will just attempt a short summary to tell you what you may expect.

In the woodlands and glens the bigger birds; rooks, tree nesting ravens and sparrowhawks are easy to spot if they are about. The conifer plantations through which the Millennium Way and Bayr ny Skeddan pass have a population of tits, goldcrest, woodcock and the long-eared owl. I camped by a plantation expecting to see these birds. I heard them, they were in good voice about four o'clock in the morning, yet I only saw a black-headed gull. On the upland moors and slopes of the mountains the curlew, snipe, skylark and meadow pipit try to steal the show, the red grouse and wheatear being less bold. I didn't see the hen harrier or the hooded crow but a kestrel was having a dispute with a few herring gulls. No doubt the owls were all peacefully asleep in their barn or local church tower. The thick stone and turf walls of the farmland, often crowned with gorse, ash or hawthorn, provide secret nesting sites for the robin, wren, pied wagtail, whitethroat and yellow hammer. As you walk through the fields in winter the visitors include fieldfare and redwing. In summer lapwing, golden plover and grey partridge are about. I got a nasty shock when a pheasant rose up under my nose with a frantic cry. It lay so well camouflaged as I was looking for the next waymark, that I nearly trod on its tail.

The Manx rivers are bright, busy streams where there are grey wagtail. Moorhens and mallard are prolific and seem to turn up on any stretch of water. Sad to tell, the dipper population has declined due to the pollution of some rivers by mining, but the good news is that the fish are returning, so perhaps the dippers will follow.

The coast provides two very different kinds of habitat. Where there are high cliffs the rocky ledges are occupied by colonies of seabirds. The dominant seabird is the herring gull, as the footpath waymark verifies, but there are other gulls and auks. Fulmar, kittiwake, guillemot, cormorant, shag, all have their favourite ledges. Razorbill and puffin like to be close to the water but the black-headed gull turns up everywhere.

The strip of land between the field edge and the cliff holds not only the footpath but a series of territories belonging to the dunnock, robin, the wren and the stonechat. I had never seen the stonechat before I camped on the Raad ny Foillan. I heard a call, 'Tea, Jack, Jack,' and on a gorse bush not a yard from the tent was this lovely little bird. It has a black head, a white collar and a chestnut breast and it spent the evening with its wife feasting on some delicacy which I did not investigate in case they flew away.

The sandy heaths of the Ayres are the nesting place of the little tern, the common tern, oystercatcher, ringed plover, and curlew.

The greatest gathering of the birds is on the intertidal mud flats where each tide invites the waders to a banquet. Oystercatchers, curlew, lapwing, golden plover, ringed plover, dunlin, sanderling, redshank and as with any party there are the gate crashers - the choughs, ducks and gulls join in too. Summer visitors can be seen resting and feeding. Sandwich terns, the red-breasted merganser and the arctic skua have been recorded breeding on the Island recently.

As you enjoy watching the birds just appreciate that it is their habitat we are visiting and it has been our pleasure to be their guests.

Turnstone

MAMMALS

The Isle of Man has few native wild mammals, yet they well represent the different habitats to be found on or around the Island.

The common and grey seal frequent the rocky inlets of the coast. The grey seal is often to be seen basking on the rocks. It is an inquisitive creature and is likely to follow you along the coast. I have been under its scrutiny many times as I walked the Raad ny Foillan.

The fields and hedgerows are frequented by the pygmy shrew, *Thollog Faiyr* its literal translation meaning 'the grass louse'. The stoat is common both in number and legend. If anyone kills a stoat it is said that revenge will soon follow.

There are three kinds of bat native to the Island, the long-eared, the natterers and the pipistrelle.

INTRODUCTION

On the moors and mountains brown and mountain hares are often seen. The Manx name for the hare is Mwaag which seems to describe its gait over the heather.

The largest native wild mammal was the Irish 'Elk', a giant deer now extinct. It was a formidable creature standing six feet high with a twelve foot span of antlers. Skeletons of the elk found on the Island are on exhibition in the Manx and Leeds Museums. It is said that its ghost can still be seen roaming the eastern glens.

The other animals on the island have been introduced, some so long ago that they have almost earned the right to be called Manx. The Loaghtan sheep was introduced from Scandinavia, its wool producing warm clothing in the times of the Vikings. It is a small agile breed and a flock roam free on the cliffs of Maughold Head. The Manx cat possesses only a tuft of hair where other cats have a tail. It was probably introduced from the mainland of Europe where other tailless cats are known to occur.

The rabbit was introduced but hedgehogs, mice and rats arrived by accident.

Of passing interest are the mainland animals which did not arrive. There are no badgers, foxes, moles or water rats. There are no snakes. Only the common and sand lizard represent the reptiles. No toads or newts are to be found and it is only recently that frogs have become established.

The Isle of Man sadly has no squirrels, but perhaps, as the red squirrel is being so hard pressed in England, a sanctuary may be offered to it one day.

Laoghtan Sheep

History

As I walked the Raad ny Foillan I was very much aware that I was walking hand in glove with history. Seeing the same scenes Celtic eyes had seen. Treading the same paths Pictish hunters had trod. Resting on the same stones where Palaeolithic man had rested, and gazing out to sea as they had gazed.

The Raad ny Foillan continually passes sites where much of Manx history occurred. There are remains of dwellings, magnificent castles, places of worship and graves of the Manx forefathers. Many excellent books and booklets, written by notable authorities (see bibliography page 141) recount the history of the Island in detail. I have tried to make a brief summary to enable the walker to recognise and appreciate the place the coastline played in the lives of these early Manx people.

Today the lives of the Islanders are closely tied to the influence of their forefathers. Their way of life makes the Isle of Man unique, and its people justly proud of their rich heritage.

The earliest archaeological remains are of Palaeolithic (Old Stone Age) man dating from 2,000 B.C. They were hunters and gatherers using flint tools. Although many such tools have been found in Britain, only one has been found in Man, discovered in the soil of Rushen Abbey.

The next arrivals were the Neolithic Picts. They were a small swarthy-skinned people, bold seafarers whose dwellings have been found on most coasts of Western Europe. Settling in the Isle of Man they followed a prosperous lifestyle as herdsmen and farmers, exercising their bold spirits by raiding Roman Britain and earning the title of the dreaded 'Painted Men'.

The Picts lived in pit dwellings. A circular hole was dug in the ground and the earth from the pit piled around it. Suitable poles were anchored on the wall and sloped inwards to form a roof. Branches were woven between the poles and covered with a thatch of reeds leaving a smoke hole in the centre.

During the construction of Ronaldsway airport a fine Pictish dwelling was discovered. Many artifacts, now in the Manx museum, lead to the opinion that the family were 'farmers, happy, prosperous and well settled.' A stone axe found in the Ronaldsway dwelling was made at the Pike o' Stickle stone axe 'factory' in Langdale, English Lake District. Five stone plaques were also

THE SIX SHEADINGS

found at Ronaldsway, the like of which have not been discovered elsewhere in the British Isles. The largest one is oval, three inches long, as thin as a penny and containing chevron and diamond patterns. Its use remains a mystery.

The Picts lived in groups or clans, the 'Bala' being the clan or family territory. The many place names beginning with Balla, merely mean 'the farm of', followed by the owner's name or the name descriptive of the territory. As time passed the Island became divided into a north and south territory, the north comprising of the 'Sheadings' of Glenfaba, Michael and Ayre, the south those of Garff, Middle and Rushen. These Pictish names remain on the maps today.

The arrival of the Celts around 200 B.C. was a most important event in the Island's history. The Celts arrived in Britain during the Bronze Age, and, being driven westward by other invaders from the continent of Europe, established themselves in Wales, Scotland, Ireland and the Isle of Man. In the Isle of Man they founded the language and the nation. The Manx language is closely related to Gaelic and is still spoken fluently by a few dedicated students. It is however, in daily use in place names, family names, ceremony and song.

The Celts brought with them the skills and techniques of smelting iron. They built many forts on hills and promontories, which suggest that times were unsettled; the hill fort on South Barrule was the most important. The Celts drove the Picts into the more barren areas of the Island but they eventually mingled to become one people.

Around the 5th century Christianity arrived with monks from Ireland. On the footpath the sites of many ancient Keeills (churches) tell of the conversion of the Island. One of these early saints was

St.Machud or Maughold who, it was said, died in 533 A.D. and was buried in Maughold churchyard. Scriptural scenes are depicted on some of the Celtic Crosses in the collection at Maunghold churchyard.

The Viking raiders first attacked Man in 798, but then the Island became 'a Viking lair' from which attacks were launched on the neighbouring coasts. In 880 Harold Haarfager included Man in his Kingdom of the Southern Isles or Sudry, and united the Isle of Man politically.

King Orry, or Gorry namely Godred Croven, after fighting against Harold at Stamford Bridge, conquered the Isle of Man. He established the Norse system of government as the national system, the Tynwald or Thingwald becoming the National Assembly, (*Thing* - an assembly, *Vollr* - a field).

The Millennium of Tynwald was celebrated in 1979 by the introduction of the long distance footpath across the Island named The Millennium Way.'

The history of the Manx Nation continued to be troubled. In 1266 the Island was sold to Scotland for 4,000 marks, Alexander II becoming Lord of Man. In 1313 Bruce attacked and captured the Scandinavian stronghold on the site where Castle Rushen now stands. It was sold yet again in 1392 to William le Scrope but he was executed by Henry IV and the Island given to Henry Percy, Duke of Northumberland. There were changes still in the wind as the Percys' rebelled against Henry and in 1403 the Island was given to John Stanley, 'in Perpetuity', on the paying of homage and two falcons to him, and every future King of England on his coronation day.

The Stanleys ruled as Kings of Man for 350 years and a settled period of history began. Sir John Stanley, who was an absentee landlord and never visited the island, appointed a governor, who in turn appointed commissioners. On Lady Day, 1423, a Tynwald court was summoned and the first Tynwald Manx 'Magna Carta' with written laws was recorded. So Tynwald and the House of Keys (the Scandinavian word *keise* meaning elected), presided over by the Governor, dealt with the legislation of the Island.

Queen Elizabeth II became Lord of Man in 1952, the Island still being governed by its own parliament which meets, according to tradition, outdoors on July 5th, the Old Midsummer Day, on the Tynwald Hill at St. John's. The foundation laid by the early settlers has moulded the Island's way of life as you see it today and provided the means of legislation for the 1961 Rights of Way Act, the Act which has completed the Raad ny Foillan for us to enjoy.

KEY TO THE MAPS

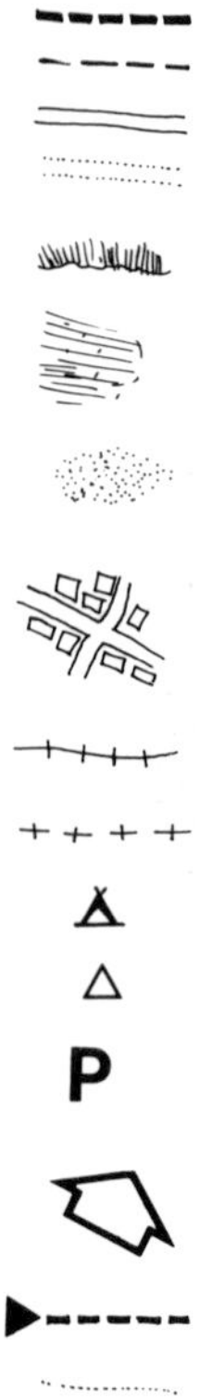

▬ ▬ ▬ ▬ ▬	The Route
▬ ▬ ▬ ▬	Other paths
═══════	Motor roads
··············	Rough lanes
ᴧᴧᴧᴧᴧᴧ	Cliffs
	Rocky beach
	Sand or pebble beach
	Village or town
┼─┼─┼─┼	Railway
+ + + +	Old railway track
Ӽ	Official camp sites
△	Hill summits
P	Car Park
	Direction of North
▶ ▬ ▬ ▬ ▬	Direction of route as described
···············	Walls or Fences
	(Only shown where necessary)

Note: (w/m) used throughout the text denotes a waymark as shown opposite

RAAD NY
FOILLAN

COASTAL FOOTPATH

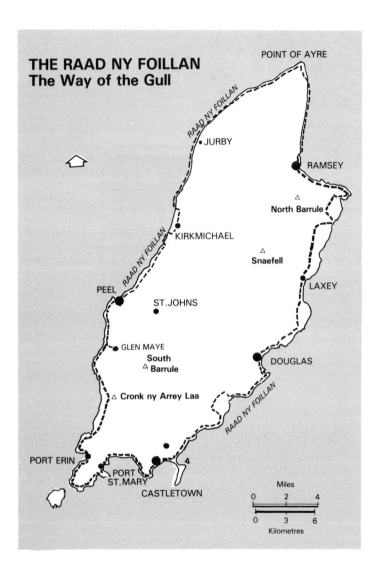

THE RAAD NY FOILLAN
The Way of the Gull

POINT OF AYRE

RAAD NY FOILLAN

• JURBY

RAMSEY

△
North Barrule

RAAD NY FOILLAN

KIRKMICHAEL

△
Snaefell

PEEL

ST.JOHNS

LAXEY

• GLEN MAYE
South
△ Barrule

DOUGLAS

△ Cronk ny Arrey Laa

RAAD NY FOILLAN

PORT ERIN

PORT
ST.MARY

CASTLETOWN

Miles
0   2   4

0   3   6
Kilometres

DOUGLAS

Tourist Information
Isle of Man Tourist Board Information Bureau,
13, Victoria Street, Douglas.
Tel: (0624) 674323 Fax: (0624) 672872
Hotels B/B
Camp Site (May-Sept) Nobles Park, Douglas.
Tel: (0624) 621132
Hot/Cold Showers.

Public Transport
BUS
Bus Station, Lord Street. Tel: 662525
Douglas - Port Erin via Oatlands Lane End, Airport,
Castletown and Port St. Mary.
Douglas - Airport
Douglas - Ramsay via Laxey
Douglas - Peel
Douglas - Ramsay via Peel and Kirk Michael
Town service via Nobles Park

STEAM TRAIN
Bank Hill Station. Tel: 663366
All stations to Port Erin.

ELECTRIC RAILWAY
Derby Castle Terminus. Tel: 663366
Douglas to Ramsay via the coast. Numerous request stops.

Services
All amenities, hospital, sea terminal,
Early closing - Thursday

Places of Interest
Manx Museum, Crellin's Hill. Tel: 675522
Manx Cattery, Nobles Park.

Douglas

DOUGLAS
to
CASTLETOWN

Distance: 15¾ miles.   Maximum height reached 300 ft.

At first glance of the map a three mile walk round the Marine Drive
may not be your idea of an unspoilt coastal path, but do not judge
hastily. In a few minutes Douglas has dropped below and the Marine
Drive is revealed as a road half way up a two hundred foot cliff where
man has failed to tame the elements. The tarmac, bombarded by rocks
from above and undermined by the sea from below, holds only the
Raad ny Foillan footpath, the impressive facade a hollow memorial to
man's grand intentions to run a tramway. If you land from the overnight boat the dawn over the sea, the rosy surf and the morning cry of
the gulls will launch you on your way in worthy style.

The wide seascapes from the Marine Drive are rivalled by the
position of this airy road, as it threads its way across the formidable
cliff face until the cliffs lower and Port Soderick is reached.

A shady glen leads inland from Port Soderick to a stretch of just over
a mile on country lanes. Return to the coast is by the fields where the

clifftop path is narrow, overgrown in places, but sound underfoot. There was only one place where the path was eroded by a spring and care required. The unspoilt coastline gives a feeling of remoteness. It is rocky with high cliffs and deep zawns. Spectacular views lie in every direction. After Cass-ny-Hawin the cliffs lower to shelving rocks and the walking becomes easier as the path widens.

At Derby Haven flocks of birds, feeding on the shallow bay, seem undisturbed by their larger noisy neighbours as they come home to roost at Ronaldsway Airport. A final road walk into Castletown gives you time to admire the situation of its fine castle.

Throughout the stage the views are excellent, gradually changing in the distance yet springing a sudden surprise near at hand.

The path is firm but the cliff is under constant erosion from the prevailing south-west wind and weather and the edge should only be approached with utmost caution.

The Route

Start at the swing bridge across the harbour in Bridge Street, where you will find the first waymark of the Raad ny Foillan. These signs, a white gull on a blue background, will guide you clockwise round the Island and return you to this spot.

Cross the swing bridge and mount the flight of steps. Turn left along the road and proceed until the Manx Radio building is on the right. Take your first break here and look back because the views across Douglas Bay are magnificent.

Entrance to the Marine Drive

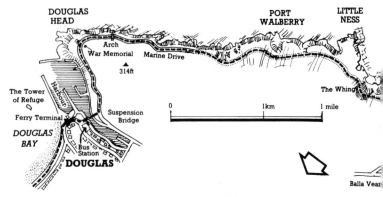

1. DOUGLAS to SANTON HEAD

Douglas is the capital of the Island; its rise to prominence being mainly due to its deep-water harbour. The underlying rock is shale so the harbour is not a victim to silting and with increasing trade the town has grown. The little isle in the bay is St. Mary's Rock with its tower of refuge. Beyond the town the patchwork of fields merges into the distant moorland of Snaefell.

Continue along the road. At the first bend is the War Memorial, then as you round the headland the scene changes.

The imposing turreted facade marks the entrance to the Marine Drive, built in 1891 it presents an uneasy partnership of brick and stone.

The bracken and heather covered moorland ends in 200 ft cliffs which fall sheer, in a deluge of crags, zawns, slides and pinnacles into the sea. The road threads its way across the face of this cliff, occupied only by the Raad ny Foillan.

The Nun's Chair

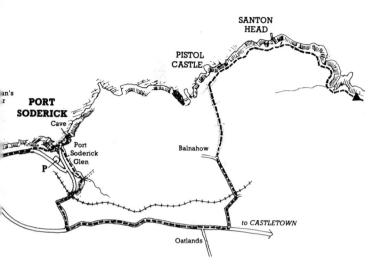

Keep to the middle of the road, out of reach of any falling stones from above. Do not go too near the edge or you may find yourself sitting down below on the rocks with other bits of fallen road. There is plenty of room for you to walk and enjoy views over the sea eastwards to Black Combe in the Lakeland hills. This is especially beautiful if you have landed from the overnight boat and dawn is creeping over the horizon. After a right bend where the road swings to pass a deep cut zawn, a detached rocky pinnacle can be seen at sea level. This is the 'Nun's Chair' where the naughty nuns from the Douglas Nunnery were put to do pennance. After passing amazing rock scenery where earth movements have folded the rocks, the cliffs become lower. At the road junction turn left.

After ¼ mile look for a footpath which veers off to the left (w/m) and descends gently at first, then more steeply by zig-zag steps to the beach at Port Soderick. Here you will find public toilets and a tap.

(Reverse Direction:- At the beach turn left. Do not pass through the Marine Drive stone arch - this path has gone - but search on its left behind an old roundabout for a well concealed flight of steps.)

A walkway round the base of the cliffs ahead leads to a little cave. You can enter this and pop out through a cleft back on the walkway.

Turn right and look for the waymark and signpost at the entrance to Port Soderick Glen.

Go through the car park and set off up the glen.

There are paths on either side of the stream which meet and cross

Port Soderick

over little footbridges. A patch of open meadow, a lovely picnic spot, is passed. Carry on through the off-set gap in a fence keeping uphill and right on a bridle path to reach a lane.

Turn left. The lane goes under a railway bridge. Keep left again to join a minor road (w/m). Turn left along the road passing a small lake formed by a dam in the Crogga River.

Follow the road until opposite Oatlands Farm. The hill to the right behind the farm is formed of Devonian granite; one of the few places where it appears on the surface. Just over the rise look for the way-mark mounted on an electricity post, which indicates a left turn into a narrower winding lane. Cross the railway bridge and climb the rise.

The railway you have just crossed is the steam railway from Douglas to Port Erin. You may have already heard a nostalgic whistle echoing over the fields but this railway is very much alive. Gleaming engines gasping noisily pull their single compartment coaches. The passengers jumping from their plush seats at every halt to peer out. Any excuse to let down the window by its leather strap.

The lane now bends towards a farm, but take the track to the right, (w/m), leading to the fields and scan the horizon for the next waymark. The track ends at a stile. Keep straight ahead through the fields and as you reach the next waymark you will be rewarded with a magnificent view of the coastline. On the left are the crags of Pistol Castle, a fine array of cliffs enjoyed by birds and rock climbers. To the right is Santon Head where the next rock strata, the Agneash Grits, come to light.

Turn right along the shy footpath.

Cliffs at Pistol Castle

This narrow footpath between the cliff edge and the fence is almost hidden in the height of summer by gorse and bracken, yet it is sound underfoot. Open balconies of turf appear and I found it idyllic to sit and enjoy the sight of the seabirds riding the air and skimming the cliff edge. Taking a break here made me feel this footpath really did belong to the gulls. Sea thrift is abundant and the tiny scarlet pimpernel I found peeping from the foot of an old wall. Yellow and blue pimpernel also grow but I have still to find them.

Continue along the footpath which winds over Santon Head, crossing the stream at Baltic Rock by a plank bridge. After passing a large telephone cable sign follow the stone wall and there is a waymark by a stile which leads down into Grenaugh Cove. Before you descend into the cove look around.

Here was the Viking fortified farm of Cronk-ny-Merrieu, protected on the seaward side by the cliff and on the landward side by a rampart with a fosse (ditch). The building was late 11th century yet when the site was excavated in 1950 traces of earlier occupation were found.

The lane gives access to the road and telephone (1 mile), and farm B&B accommodation (see Page 11).

Leave the bay by crossing the site of the old building. The path slants upwards to gain the cliff edge again on the opposite side of the cove. From here to Port Soldrick the path lies between the cliff edge

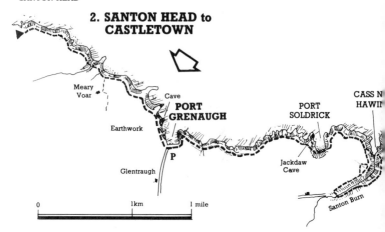

2. SANTON HEAD to CASTLETOWN

Meary Voar

Cave

PORT GRENAUGH

Earthwork

PORT SOLDRICK

CASS N HAWII

P

Glentraugh

Jackdaw Cave

Santon Burn

0   1km   1 mile

and the field, but in places it is overgrown or eroded and it is necessary to alternate between the cliff and the field.

At a kissing gate enter the field for a short while, then return to the cliff edge at the next gate. A little spring is passed, then a return into the neighbouring field keeping to the seaward edge, where a gate returns you to the cliff edge once more.

The path continues to wind between the field and the cliff top until a squat cove, Port Soldrick, is reached. Here the path divides allowing you to choose your route. You can either skirt the cove by a circle of the cove rim along an indistinct path which is much overgrown, or make a descent into the cove.

The descent is better. When level with the beach continue straight ahead by a path up the other side cut through a tunnel of vegetation. On reaching the cliff top a fine sea cave on the east side of the cove can be seen and the views are splendid back to Santon Head and forward to Langness and Castletown.

Caves on the coastline bring to mind smugglers and this is Jackdaw cave, a genuine smugglers' hideout. Boats entered the cave and were secretly loaded through a hole in the roof. Around the year 1700 the Island was being used as a 'trading' centre for brandy. Manx merchants would buy brandy and silks from France and rum from Jamaica. The goods were then brought to the Isle of Man duty free in the fast Manx clippers. This was quite legal. The same clippers then ran cargoes to quiet coves on the Welsh, Cheshire, Lancashire, Scottish and Irish coasts.

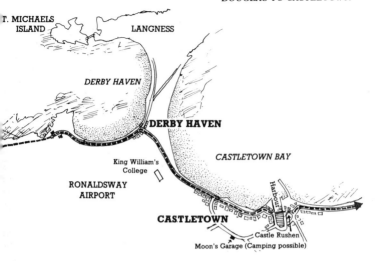

The Manx were skilful sailors knowing every inch of the Irish sea and the British revenue cutters were continually outmanoeuvred. The smugglers have gone and so have the jackdaws. Housemartins are the present tenants.

In a short while you will pass Cass-ny-Hawin Head and approach the deep inlet of Cass-ny-Hawin where the Santon Burn enters the sea. Across the inlet the rocky knoll with sea caves at its foot and an earthwork on top is your objective.

Do not lose any height as a decision has to be made here. If the tide is out and the Santon Burn is not in flood it is possible to easily wade the stream and gain the cliff top by an obvious path, but if you do not want to get your feet wet, take the path ahead. A path is cut through the dense gorse close to the field and overlooking the edge of the ravine. At the time of writing the cut path is not complete and you have to take to the field on the right. Pass through a gate diagonally right and return to the left-hand side of the field. Pass through another gate. Continue past a trough following the side of the field until a gate leads to a sunken lane. Turn left to a footbridge over the Santon Burn.

Turn left following the valley downstream for a short way to enter a field. Descend to pass through a gate and continue in the valley to another gate, the inlet being on the left. Follow the line of a stone wall until a three-way signpost and waymark are seen. (Ignore an old foot-path sign half hidden amongst the bushes on the field side of the wall.) Cross a small stream and continue on a rising path through the gorse

41

until you reach the cliff top field, the junction of the 'waders' path and the site of the ancient fort of Cass-ny-Hawin.

Now turn right and follow the coast past a forlorn gate. The cliff gradually lowers and the easy path gives you chance to look around. The quarry on your right announces a change of rock to the Carboniferous limestone. It is a working quarry, the rock being used for roadstone. Pass by the gantry which holds the landing lights for Ronaldsway Airport. Across the shallow bay of Derby Haven St. Michael's Island attracts the eye.

The Island is joined to Langness by a causeway and the ruin of St. Michael's chapel stands a silhouette against the sea. The chapel was built on the site of an ancient Celtic keeill, the round fort being erected about 1540. The tall tower on Langness (1800) is impressive but its original purpose remains uncertain. A watchtower against the fleet of Napoleon or a beacon tower are the most popular theories. If the tide is on the turn, Derby Haven becomes a birdwatchers' paradise as all the seabirds in the area are attracted to a feast of wriggling goodies. To be seen are:- duck, curlew, plover, dunlin, lapwing, redshank, wigeon, snipe and curlew sandpiper. In winter bar-tailed godwit and the choughs.

At Derby Haven turn right at the telephone box.

The narrow neck of land between Derby Haven and Castletown Bay is Ronaldswath or Ronald's Way. Boats were hauled across the isthmus to avoid the difficult tide race round Langness. King Ronald laid a paved way to make the task easier. Langness Light on Dreswick Point, one of the four Manx lighthouses, guards this section of the coast.

Follow the road round the bay into Castletown.

On the right the buildings of King William's College demand your attention. A fund begun by Bishop Barrow in the 17th century provided grants for deserving pupils and in 1830 a general appeal by the Governor to add to these funds resulted in the building of this well-known public school; King William IV was approached for a donation, but as he had no money at the time he gave it his name instead! The new building was unfortunately destroyed by fire in 1844 with the loss of many valuable documents. Public subscription was again generous and the fine building of local limestone is the one you see today.

Guillemot

Castletown from Scarlett Point

CASTLETOWN

Tourist Information
Town Hall, Parliament Square. Tel: (0624) 823518

Accommodation
Hotel, B&B,
B&B Mrs. Jelley, The Rowens, Douglas St.,
Castletown. 823210
Camp Site (marked on the map) but NOTE no camping
allowed for walkers
Camping - Moon's Garage (Esso), Victoria Road,
Castletown

Public Transport
Bus - Castletown - Airport, Douglas, Port St. Mary,
Port Erin, Peel
Steam Train - Stations to Douglas, Port Erin

Services
Full range of shops. Market Day - Thursday morning June-
August
Swimming Pool

Places of Interest
Castle Rushen, The Nautical Museum. The original House
of Keys, Scarlett Nature Trail Visitors' Centre.

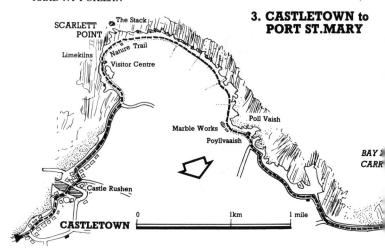

CASTLETOWN
to
PORT ST. MARY

Distance: 6¾ miles at sea level

A very easy and fast section. Road walking gives way to a track with views back to Castletown, Derby Haven and Langness Point. From Scarlett Point a smooth grassy path is on gently shelving turf along a low rocky shore line. This is part of the Scarlett Nature Trail.

The extensive seascape panoramas are captivating and continually changing. The coast from Langness to Spanish Head and the Calf of Man is on view. There is a stretch of road walking from Poyllvaaish to Rhenwyllan then a good footpath and the firm sand of Chapel Bay leads to Port St. Mary.

The Route

The focal point of Castletown is the market square. On market day it is a hive of activity and you have to thread your way through the stalls to leave the square by the S.W. corner. The road soon divides and on a 'no through road' signpost the Raad ny Foillan waymark will be seen.

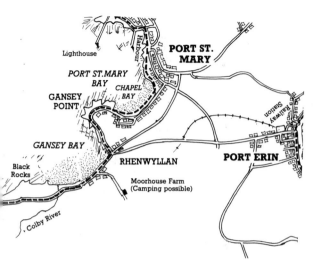

The coast road is then followed. On the shore there are more birds to be seen. Look for a heron, almost invisible, patiently fishing. There may be other waders and the golden-eye - a neat little black and white duck, the male having a black-green head, the female a chestnut - they look as though they are wearing a woolly balaclava. The coast road soon turns left to a track along the edge of the bay towards Scarlett Point.

The water-filled quarry on your right was once a major industry. Limestone for building was loaded into ships from the jetty, the remains of which are on your left. The quarry closed at the end of the 19th century after supplying stone for the southern branch of the Isle of Man Railway. As you pass the quarry, spare a moment to look at the fine view of Castletown. Opposite the southern end of the quarry, at sea level, are three lime kilns. It is well worth the scramble down the slope to view these at close quarters.

Back on the path is the Scarlett Visitors' Centre. There is a nature trail round Scarlett Point. In fact you have already walked some of it.

The small booklet published by the Manx Conservation Trust is full of information and is excellent value. It is available from the Centre or from the local Information Offices.

The path is through soft turf sprinkled with an array of limestone-loving flowers that are willing to tolerate the salty atmosphere - thyme, sea thrift, bird's-foot trefoil, stonecrop and sea spurrey. As you

45

Old limekilns at Scarlett Point

progress along the rocky shore views open to the west. On a clear day you can see the old Chicken Rock Lighthouse 6½ miles away and the Burroo Rock, the large rock with the natural arch off the southern tip of the Calf of Man.

As Port St. Mary and Spanish Head come into sight a stile and a waymark confirm the way.

Scarlett Point takes its name from Skarfakluft, the norse word meaning cormorant's cleft. The most southerly rock of the point is the Stack, its basalt ledges being a favourite perch for cormorants, shags, auks and gulls.

Scarlett Point was also one of the 'Day Watch Hills'. Documents from the Scandinvian period of 1627 tell of the duty of Ward and Watch. Men were obliged to report from sunrise to sunset 'For serious duty and properly armed'.

Continue along the path perhaps making brief excursions to examine the lichens which grow on the rocks. (See section on Flora page 21.) Poyllvaaish quarry and its workshop are soon passed on the right.

The limestone of this quarry has been metamorphosed (heated by volcanic contact) three times. Today it is cut and polished for fancy goods and paving stones. Stone steps of Poyllvaaish marble were the Island's contribution to the building of St. Paul's Cathedral. When the steps became worn they were retired to an upstairs gallery.

Lichens grow profusely. Here are 'Ramalina Siliquosa' and 'Lecanora Atra'.

After passing the workshop the path changes to a track. Ignore a signpost showing a footpath returning to Castletown over the fields. Go straight on through the farmyard and onto the road, (w/m). This road soon joins the main road from Castletown to Port St. Mary. Turn left towards Port St. Mary, (w/m). A section of road-walking is now necessary but it is not as tedious as may be suspected. The pavement is on the seaward side and extensive views and perchance a performance of water skiers, enhance the plod. At the pub where the Colby road turns right, a major fault line changes the strata and the Barrule Slates appear once more.

Continue past the road branching right to Port Erin and at Rhenwyllan look for a waymark where the footpath turns left. The footpath passes by a group of pretty cottages then after rounding the point you can choose to walk along the beach or on the pavement round Chapel Bay to Port St. Mary. The town clings to the hillside and a flight of steps leads up through gardens to the town. To continue the Raad ny Foillan stay at sea level and after passing through the gardens a raised walkway leads past fishing cottages to the picturesque harbour.

PORT ST. MARY

Tourist Information
Town Hall, Promenade. Tel: (0624) 832101

Accommodation
Hotel, B&B
Camping - Moorhouse Farm - Gansey Bay

Public Transport
Bus - Port Erin, Castletown, Douglas, Peel
Buses run from the harbour
Trains - Stations to Douglas, Port Erin

Services
Full range of shops. Late shopping to 9.00pm. Mondays.
Early closing Thursday.

Places of Interest
Cregneish Village Folk Museum. Open early May-late September. Weekdays and Sunday afternoons.
Mull Hill stone circle

The raised walkway at Port St. Mary

Port St. Mary

PORT ST. MARY
to
PORT ERIN

Distance: 7 miles.   Maximum height reached: 400ft.

This section of the Raad ny Foillan is a casket of pleasure, from which I sample memories by the fireside on long winter evenings.

From the map it may appear to be just a quick two hour stroll but it is a section on which to linger. After leaving Port St. Mary the way passes Kallow Point then, rising round Perwick Bay, joins a quiet lane. The lane rises steeply then is left behind as you enter the Manx National Trust area for Public Ramblage, The Chasms. The footpath circles high above The Chasms and Bay Stacka where the views are breathtaking. The footpath is sound and clearly marked but **extreme caution must be exercised. Children and dogs must be strictly supervised.** The grass changes to moorland and the path narrows as it passes Black Head and Spanish Head. The Calf of Man and its Sound dominate the view to the west. The Calf Sound and its treacherous tide race draws many sightseers, but their presence warrants a café and toilets. The footpath then takes a rising traverse passing Aldrick,

49

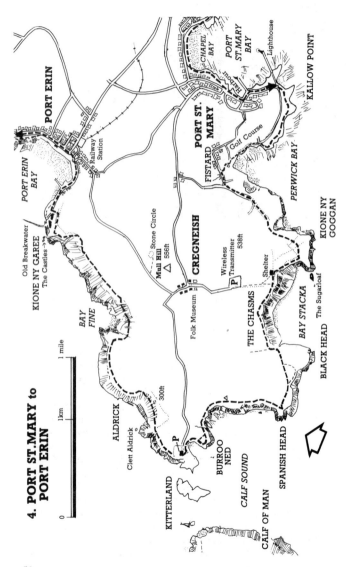

4. PORT ST.MARY to PORT ERIN

The Burroo Rock, off the Calf of Man

and onto the open moor high above Bay Fine, until a descent is made into the sheltered bay of Port Erin.

A worthwhile excursion can be made to Cregneish, a traditional Manx village maintained as a Folk Museum and the Mull Hill Circle, a neolithic monument unique in Britain in its fine state of preservation.

The Route

To continue the Raad ny Foillan turn left from the waymark at the south-west corner of the harbour and stroll along the side of the harbour, sampling its nautical flavour and sea-borne smells. Turn right along Lime Street.

In the sea-food factory on the right scallops and queenies are prepared for export. Scallops are bivalves. They swim about by flapping strong valves attached to their two pink and white ribbed shells. It is whilst they are swimming that they are caught by the local fishermen. As one sailor bemoaned whilst I watched him mend his nets, 'Catches are bad. The sea hasn't warmed up yet and the queenies are all in bed'. The scallops are sent to Europe and the smaller queenies to the U.S.A.

At the lifeboat station is a waymark where you can leave the road. Use the footpath along the sea wall to Kallow Point. Now you can enjoy the expanding views eastwards to Langness Point, westwards to The Chasms. Pass a colonnaded shelter, then as the footpath nears the road, move onto the road and continue on a track ahead, (w/m). A

51

post stile gives access to a concrete path which mounts between the golf course and the edge of the now heightening cliffs. Do not take the small path on the left which leads down to the shore, but keep on the paved path. A gate gives onto the road, turn left to a hotel gate with a 'No Through Road' notice. The Raad ny Foillan waymark is your passport, so pass through. Keep to the right through the hotel grounds until an enclosed pathway on the right takes you between high hedges, to a kissing gate (w/m) opening onto a narrow lane. Turn left down the lane and cross Glenchass Bridge. Ignore the lane on the left and continue up the hill where a finger post signs you to The Chasms.

As the gradient eases the views unfold. At a junction keep straight on (w/m). The path is now along a pleasant green walled track leading into a pasture. You are now in the National Trust area of Public Ramblage. Please observe the countryside code and leave this wild and beautiful area as you discovered it. Over the cliff edge is Kione-y-Ghoggan (The Anvil) a favourite breeding spot for guillemots, kittiwakes and puffins.

The exit to the field is diagonally left. Next make your way diagonally right almost to the point where the grass ends at the dizzy edge of The Chasms. The wall ends in a protected balcony with a kissing gate. You are on the edge of the cliff.

IF VISIBILITY IS POOR On leaving the field turn right. Stay close by the wall. It will lead you uphill then will turn you left until you come to the protected balcony and kissing gate. Turn right.

Large rocks provide a good seat from which to view the seabirds. Guillemots, razorbills, fulmars, petrels, shags, kittiwakes and other gulls nest here. Choughs like the security of The Chasms' cracks for their nests, and ravens are regular visitors. Directly below lies the Sugarloaf, the Island's finest sea stack. It was first climbed in 1933 by Dr. A.W.Kelly, one of the pioneer rock climbers on the Island. He approached by boat and climbed the stack alone. There have been few subsequent ascents, for the rock is loose and lubricated with bird droppings.

The Chasms are great rifts in the earth caused by severe earth movements. They vary in width from several feet to a few inches, in depth they split the rocks to below sea level. The fissures are overgrown with heather and other vegetation so be safe, stay on the path.

Go through the kissing gate. Keep close to the left-hand side of the fence and mount rocky steps for about 50yds, until a stile crosses the fence and the path takes the right-hand side of the wall to an old building. This building was the old Chasms Café. It may not look attractive but it has a seat and provides shelter.

The footpath comes very close to the cliff edge at The Chasms, overlooking the Sugarloaf.

Excursion to Cregneish and Mull Hill

From the old Chasms café the path leads uphill towards a car park at the radio beacon. Go through the car park and straight along the narrow lane to the old Manx village of Cregneish. The thatched cottages have been preserved and furnished by the Manx Museum and National Trust as a Folk Museum. You can obtain a ticket from Cullan Beg, one of the more modern houses, which will entitle you to an enlightening chat in the various cottages. If closed it is still worth walking round the village and peeping in the windows. To visit the Mull Hill Stone Circle, take the uphill road through the village to the main road. At the main road leading to the Sound turn left, then take the next fork right along the minor road signed Port Erin. On the right just beyond a stony track, a path slants up the hillside. At the top of the hill is the stone circle of Mull Hill. The Meayll or Mull Circle is a Neolithic monument unique in Great Britain. Its ancient name is Rhullick-y-lag-sliggagh or 'The graveyard of broken slates'. This is a remarkable late Neolithic burial ground situated just below the ruins of Pictish villages. Originally it was a Round Barrow containing six sets of graves, each set consisting of three stone chambers arranged in a fifty foot diameter circle. Urns containing human ashes, flint heads, scrapers, knives and small pottery vessels which had once contained food were found inside. C.W.Airne in his book The Story of the Isle of Man *poses the question 'Why did the Picts who grew wheat on Mull Hill cremate their dead and bury their ashes in a round barrow?' One thing we do know, they chose a most wonderful viewpoint.*

54   *One of the six pairs of kists, burial chambers, at Mull Hill*

(We now return to the main route description)

On leaving the shelter bear left to the fell corner - National Trust sign.

Over the stile and straight ahead the path threads its way through the heath. To the right the automatic wireless transmitting direction-finding station can be seen. Ignore the stile leading right by an obsolete finger post and continue descending the narrow track on the cliff edge. Cross a small stream soon then climb up over the hill onto Spanish Head. (An alternative path forks left on the moor just below the top.) At this point there is a path junction, the main path forks left over the shoulder to gain the cliff edge. Follow this and as you pass through a rocky gateway the Chicken Rock Lighthouse and the Calf of Man can be seen.

Why Chicken Rock? Allow me to quote from Kingsley's The Water Babies *and you will have the answer. 'There came by a flock of petrels who said, 'we are Mother Carey's own chickens, she sends us out all over the seas to show the good birds the way home'. The petrels still come home to the Calf of Man.*

The path now goes along the cliff top then descends to cross a small ghyll. Tourists take a short cut from here across the field to the car park, but if you turn left after crossing the ghyll a finger post directs the way clockwise, round the knoll where you will be rewarded by a prime viewpoint over the Sound. Continue past the memorial to Sir Percy Cowley, a Manxman who unlocked the gate leading to the open countryside we now enjoy. Raise your pot of tea to him in the Sound Café. (Car park and toilets here.)

The Calf of Man is separated from its parent by the Sound and is now a National Trust area open for Public Ramblage. There is a bird observatory which offers day facilities and accommodation to the birdwatcher. Daily visits are arranged from Port Erin and those who wish to stay longer can apply to the Isle of Man Tourist Board, Douglas, for details. Many birds nest there but alas it has been almost abandoned by the Manx shearwater. In 1786 rats escaped from the wreck of a Russian ship. They attacked the helpless fledglings and the colony was abandoned by the birds. They have rarely been seen since.

Other tales of woe were attached to the Calf. The Chicken Rock Light-house was badly damaged by fire in 1960. It now houses an automatic light and fog signal.

Many ships have come to grief in the Sound. The passage is encumbered with rocks and the tidal currents meet resulting in overfalls and eddies. I once had the pleasure of looking round a naval survey vessel. We were shown the latest job in hand which was a chart of the Sound of Man. It

The Thousla Cross overlooking The Sound

looked like a grand canyon with pinnacles of jagged rock, caves, holes and fissures. Spectacular to see but needing the skill of 'Manannan Mac Lir, a celebrated merchant of the Isle of Man, who was the best pilot living in Western Europe' to navigate. So says an ancient Irish manuscript of 900A.D.

To the north of the café stands the Thousla Cross. It stands in memory of the local men who lost their lives in the rescue of the crew of the French Schooner Jeane St. Charles in 1858.

Pass the Thousla Cross. Beyond it a stile gives access to open grassy slopes. (w/m and finger post). The path climbs the grass slope to a green balcony. Look up leftwards above a collection of boulders to the horizon where a finger post can be seen. The path rises and another finger post comes into view as you gain height. The path then curves leftwards along the green balcony and passes through the boulders to reach a stile by the finger post which you spotted on the horizon. The footpath has gained the 200ft. contour. Far below are the crags of Bay Fine, the breeding place for a colony of black guillemots. The path wanders between the fence and the cliff top, its position giving views of the Calf of Man. If the tide race is in full flow you will hear why it is called 'The Sound'. Bradda Head with the Milner Tower now dominate the scene to the north.

Aldrick

Another stile and finger post is passed and an assortment of rising sheep tracks on the open moor lead to another finger post. Continue on a rising path until, as you round the shoulder of the moor, Port Erin comes into view. The path now descends gently, bending right as it follows a wall. A wire fence bars the way but there is a gate at its seaward end. The path hugs the fence then turns sharp right through a gate (finger post). A sheltered pathway between fence and wall leads to Port Erin.

Before you dash for the nearest refreshment pause for a while. Over the wall is the favourite gossiping spot of the Port Erin gulls, here you have the chance to study them at very close quarters. This is indeed the way of the gull.

Descend to the harbour by a flight of steps on the left.

The building on your left is the Marine Biological Research Laboratory run by Liverpool University. Toilets on the right with tap.

Boat trips to the Calf of Man leave from the harbour daily (weather permitting). These are working boats. If you take a trip you may return accompanied by lobsters and richer for the interesting conversation with the Port Erin fishermen.

The road past the harbour leads to the telephone boxes by the beach where the next section starts.

Port Erin

PORT ERIN
Tourist Information
Commissioner's Office, Station Road. Tel: (0624) 832298

Accommodation
Hotels, B&B
Ballacallen Hotel - Dalby. Tel: 842030
Keggan, The Gables, 3 Glen Close, Glen Maye. Tel: 844023

Public Transport
Bus Depot Station. Tel: 833125
Port Erin   - Douglas via Port St. Mary, Castletown, Airport
 - Peel via Castletown, Airport, Ballasalla, Foxdale, St. Johns.
 - Cregneish and the Sound
Steam Trains - Stations to Douglas. Daily except Saturday.

Services
Full range of shops. Early closing Thursday.

Places of Interest
Marine Biological Station and Aquarium.
Boat trips round the Calf of Man. Bird watching visits to the Calf of Man.
Steam Railway Museum.

PORT ERIN
to
PEEL

Distance: 14½ miles.   Maximum height reached: 1,434 ft.

This is a mountain section over the Carnanes with three summits, - Bradda Hill, Lhiattee ny Beinee and Cronk ny Arrey Laa, each one higher, wilder and more remote than its predecessor. The western side of each hill plunges in sheer cliffs to the sea giving views to which I cannot do justice. If the visibility is poor serious thought should be given to using the lower level alternative way to the east. (see map pages 60 and 61) Map and compass essential.

The road walk along the promenade, although short and attractive, can be further improved by taking the traversing path, part-way down the cliff. You are soon onto open pastures which change to wild moorland. Superb views unfold as height is gained to the Milner Tower. The traverse over Bradda Head is on good paths, yet wild and magnificent, ending in a steep descent to Fleshwick Bay.

The ascent of Lhiattee ny Beinee rises steeply from Fleshwick Bay. On leaving the intake wall the way is across trackless moorland on the seaward side of a broad ridge where the atmosphere is wild and the views exciting. A steep descent is made to The Sloc, where the road is approached but not used.

The ascent of Cronk ny Arrey Laa is on a well trodden path until the shoulder below the summit is reached. The way is now virgin moor over the summit (1434ft.), the highest point reached by the Raad ny Foillan, and down to Glion Mooar. Magnificent panoramas are in every direction. A section of road (1 mile) is followed by a return to the coast. A short visit to Glen Maye leads to coastal meadowland until the traverse round Corrin's Hill and onto Peel Hill brings the grand finale, the sudden display of St. Patrick's Isle with its ancient castle.

The Route

There are two ways to leave Port Erin so start by the waymark near the telephone boxes on the lower promenade. From this point as you face the sea turn right and make your decision. The *official* way takes the higher promenade until you see the waymark on your left. A gate opens onto a green path sandwiched between a wall and a fence. This

59

5. PORT ERIN to CREGGANMOAR

path is soon joined from the left by the Coronation footpath to Bradda Head. At this point the other way from Port Erin meets the Raad ny Foillan.

The alternative is:

From the telephone boxes walk a few yards north along the beach where the freshwater spring of St. Catherine's Well can be seen. It was this spring which first attracted seafarers to this sheltered bay. Go up the steps by the side of the Well and turn left along the lower promenade between the houses and their sea-side gardens. Fuschia grows in profusion and is one of the bonuses of a summer visit. A longer flight of steps takes you to the level of the upper promenade. Do not walk far along the pavement but take to the lawns on its left where a paved walkway begins. You follow this walkway left as it threads its way along the face of the vegetated cliff. Continue past the old swimming pool, a relic of the past. Do not take the upward way to the road but keep traversing the cliff path round the next cove. You will soon arrive at the Bradda Glen café. Walk straight on through the grounds. (Or ask yourself if you have come far enough to justify a fine Manx ice cream.) After the café a signpost 'Coronation Footpath' points to the right. Follow this path through a gap in the wall and you are on the Raad ny Foillan again.

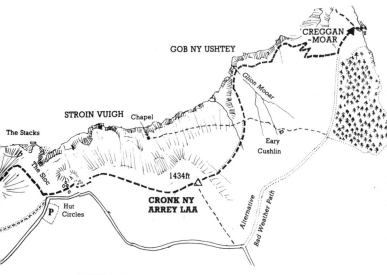

St. Catherine's Well, Port Erin

The Milner Tower on Bradda Head

Turn left along the green path which gradually gains height, the view improving with every step. The path widens, bending right to join the main path from the car park, then swings back left until the last steeper climb takes you to the doorway of the Milner Tower. You can climb the spiral staircase to the viewing platform.

If you look away across the sea to the south you may see Manannin Isle. This Isle, it is said in legend, rises above the waves on Midsummer Day every seventh year. A strange boat brings an assortment of enchanted fairy folk to Port Erin. Do not get entangled with them, or you will have to accompany them to their water home under the sea. There you will have to work for the Sea King until Midsummer Day seven years hence.

William Milner was a Liverpool safe maker. About the year 1864 he was active in the erection of a breakwater to shelter the bay from the westerly winds and make a harbour of refuge for the fishermen. When the foundation stone was laid he threw a great party for the whole neighbourhood. In gratitude and respect for their benefactor the tower was built during his lifetime. It was built in the shape of one of his earlier keys.

From the tower descend the way you came a hundred yards, then leave the car park path turning right (28°E) passing the spot where the world's winning photograph was taken (see plaque on tower). Next pass an old mine building, cross a stile and continue on the right of the fence and spoil heaps. If you scratch around, pieces of pyrite (fool's gold) can be found. Copper, lead and silver were mined here until approx. 1880. The path now follows the cliff top, gaining height towards Bradda Hill. As the path rises and the height above the sea increases you are treated to dramatic glimpses of the surf far below. The grass gives way to bracken and heather as the path climbs in two stages to its highest point. From here a small track on the right leads to the summit cairn 726ft. The path continues on its way past the summit and another small track from the cairn will take you back onto it completing a short triangular diversion. The path now heads in an easterly direction towards Fleshwick Bay. Cross the wall at the Public Right of Way sign.

Note: It would be an advantage at this spot to survey the route ahead. Look for the point where the intake wall from Fleshwick Bay turns a right angle south and the Raad ny Foillan bears left diagonally up the untracked ridge of Lhiattee ny Beinee.

Descend the steep zig-zag path down the bracken slopes, between the plantation and the coast, (a minor crag is avoided by one of the descending traverses of the path). A gate leads into a field. Cross the field to the road, (w/m).

Note: The Isle of Man Public Rights of Way and Leisure Map shows the path going through the plantation. There is a right of way through the plantation but it is seldom used. The trees will afford you shade but will deny you the chance to enjoy the view down into Fleshwick Bay.

Turn left down the road to the beach.

Fleshwick Bay, derived from the Scandinavian Fles-vik or green creek, is a favourite haunt of scuba divers. The surrounding cliffs turn this little bay into a suntrap and the clear water made me want to take a dip myself. I quickly changed my mind when the wet-suited divers returned saying they would come back later in the year when the water had warmed up!

The waymark on the finger post by the beach invites you to jump across the stream and set off up the rough grass covered slope towards a beckoning second finger post. The path is no more than an ant track which passes through gorse as it crosses the head of a deep cut zawn. At the second finger post you encounter a boggy area. Either frog hop ahead then climb the intake fence by a wall junction or squelch across left to a third finger post and stile. Gain the side of the wall and follow it to join a way made by the fence climbers. Follow the smooth dry path now running parallel to the stone wall just left of dense bracken, until the wall turns off to the right at a corner.

Note: that the blue route line on the map does not follow the way-marked route but goes through the farm and field to join our description where the intake fence can be climbed.

Fleshwick Bay

From your position near the wall corner the moor rising up ahead looks trackless and the short gorse uninviting. Until a path is worn, look upon yourself as a pioneer and put your best foot forward.

Bear left almost horizontally until you cross the level of an old pony track, keeping to the border of the grass and the gorse. Discover a sheep track which will make the going easier until you arrive at two prominent rocks. Turn right and soldier upwards to pass a low crag on its left to gain a broad ridge. Contour left until you cross a broken fence and continue a gently rising traverse.

A view of the previously unseen face of Bradda Head comes into sight.

The way now becomes more distinct. At the highest point of the cliff you can take a break and if the visibility is good identify on the western horizon the Mountains of Mourne sweeping down to the sea.

In September this moor is a carpet of colour. The purple of the heather mixed with the bright yellow of the late summer flowering short gorse is a sight to see, mingled here and there by patches of white cotton grass. (Not really a grass but a sedge.)

Pass a cairn and keep on the edge overlooking the coast. Cross the remains of an old wall.

A brief excursion nearer the edge will enable you to gain view of a new panorama north. Extending into the sea is the rock spit of Niarbyl (the tail

Cronk ny Arrey Laa from Lhiattee ny Beinee

of the rocks) and beyond Corrin's Hill near Peel can be seen.

Continue along the intermittent path to the large cairn which occupies the summit of Lhiattee ny Beinee, 988ft.

The cairn forms a circular wind shelter from which to view the panorama. Circling from east to west you can see the Manx radio mast at Douglas, the south-east coast, Ronaldsway, the Langness Peninsula, Scarlett Point, the Calf of Man and Bradda Head. On a very clear day it is possible to see the Lancashire hills to the east, the Irish mountains to the west and peeping over the southern horizon the Welsh mountains.

A tiny cairn to the N.E. 40°E sets the way. Slant left to meet the cliff top path and follow the broad ridge. This soon steepens and the path evaporates. Make a springy descent through the heather to a waymark on a signpost at The Sloc, the gap between the two hills. Go over the stile and turn right along the wall to the next signpost (w/m). In front, through the sheep pen, is the road, car park and picnic area.

From the signpost (w/m) by the sheep enclosure set off N.E. on a prominent path which traverses the base of a small hill. Keep straight ahead to a gate in the fence. You now take a rigid line for the summit of Cronk ny Arrey Laa, held by a severe path policed with white-topped posts each with its official right-of-way badge. When you have gained a few hundred feet turn and look back.

The flat top of the small hill now reveals an ancient earthwork, the site of a Pictish village where Neolithic farmers tilled the land. They feared tribal raids when times were hard and built a stronghold on the crown of the hill, surrounded by a ditch with pointed stakes and hurling stones. Little of this remains but the outlines of their pit dwellings, the walls being built of stone slabs, can clearly be seen today.

65

Lhiattee ny Beinee from Cronk ny Arrey Laa. The site of a Pictish village can be seen on the small hill in the centre.

The path is steep and the name of the hill Cronk ny Arrey Laa - Hill of the Morning Watch, gives food for thought until you notice a sudden change of gradient. The tourists must notice this change too and unwilling to lose sight of the car park they call it a day. With their return to security, the path ends. Keep straight on over the short heather, the line of your right of way indicated by the posts, until you reach the huge summit cairn 1434ft.

A metal notice tells that this is no ordinary cairn but a prehistoric burial mound probably of the early Bronze Age about 1500BC. It has been excavated and its summit restored in 1958. Cronk ny Arrey Laa was a Day Watch hill as were the other hills on the western side of the Island. The watchman in his position of trust could look out as you can now, over the southern half of Man, spread at his feet. Papers in Castle Rushen dated 1627 set out the punishments for failure to turn up, or going to sleep on duty. For the first duty failed the watchman must 'Forfiet bodye and goodes'. For the second failure the 'Forfiet' was 'a cowe'. The third time 'Lyfe and Lyme to yr Lorde', sounded nasty. It was the poor widows I felt sorry for. Because of the wind the 'widdows of the island' had to 'gather fuel for fires for warmth and the beacon'. I wonder who carried it to the top?

From the cairn a major path descends east to the nearby road but the Raad ny Foillan does not take it. Our route aims north towards,

66

yet does not pass, a white farmhouse, Eary Cushlin, now an outdoor centre. (Note the line of the rough lane on the right of the white farmhouse. A bad weather alternative can be used by taking the major path east to the road. Turn left, then left again where the road bends off right. This lane can now be followed to join the Raad ny Foillan at Cregganmoar.)

Proceed a few yards from the cairn in a northerly direction and an east-west wall comes into view crossing the hillside below. Our route aims to cross this wall then follow the northward low wall which joins it. The descent to the wall is very steep through untracked heather and bilberry. A small rocky outcrop and occasional boulders across your way demand caution and a controlled, careful descent is called for.

Cross the horizontal wall barring your way at a T-junction with the low wall. A grassy track on the right of the low wall is the path. Keep following this path, merely a sheep track, by the low wall until it bends left towards the sea. Go through a gap in an earth bank and continue down soft turf still by the low wall. Another gap in an earth bank is reached. Cross the pony track which goes left to an old keeill, and right to Eary Cushlin. A few yards right along this track is a stream: five minutes further, a spring. Camping possibility for back-packers.

The track leads to Keeill Lag-ny-Keeilley. The Keeill was a little church built approx. 430-700AD on a small natural platform in the steep hillside. It had a foundation of stone with walls of sods and brushwood roofed with thatch. It was rectangular - 15ft. by 10ft. - having a window to the east and a door to the west. The hermit-priest lived in a small hut close by the well and field which he cultivated. The chapel was last used for a funeral a hundred years ago. The body was strapped to the back of a pony and the mourners followed on foot.

The low wall is now covered with bracken, continue to follow it. Glancing back, it may have crossed your mind that the way of the gull has turned into the way of the grouse, but as you continue to descend the sound of the sea and a welcome signpost (w/m) confirm that you are still on the Raad ny Foillan.

Sit on the last remains of the low wall and enjoy the quiet charm of this remote bay, guarded by the fragile heather from the busy excursionist.

The path now turns right along the coast and descends into the small valley of Glion Mooar. Cross the fence and jump the stream below the wire fence. Descend a little and the path rises round a shoulder and continues through bracken. A high ladder stile (w/m) allows you to see a fork in the velvet turf path. Take the upper path

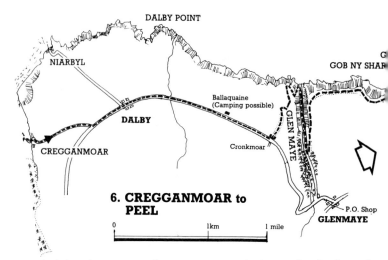

6. CREGGANMOAR to PEEL

(w/m) and as you wend your way upwards say a quiet thanks to the owner who cares for the footpath so splendidly.

At the Manx National Trust sign *Creggan Moar Brooghs* pass through a gateway and turn left down a bridle track. (The alternative route rejoins at this point.) The bridle track is crossed by an old lane. Keep straight on down this lane which has the air of a rocky *wadi*. It soon narrows and you pop through a gate into another more civilised lane. Cross the ford at Cregganmoar and bend right up the surfaced road and over the cattle grid. Ignore the signpost pointing right. Continue along the narrow road until you must turn left along the main road.

The unfortunate road walk lasts for just over a mile. (A lane branching left at Dalby, its junction marked by a telephone box, leads to Niarbyl Bay. This bay with its tail of rocks and thatched cottages is an attraction. The tail is a ridge of rock protruding into the sea, where the Niarbyl and Lonan flags terminate with a flourish.)

At the hamlet of Cronkmooar look on the left for a tiny lane between two cottages. Signpost (w/m). Turn left down the lane, through a five-barred gate into an enclosed pathway. Follow the right of way signs through the fields to the coast. The path now descends right into the rocky outlet of Glen Maye. Signpost (w/m).

The footbridge over the stream leads to a pretty rocky cove with a limekiln-like shelter.

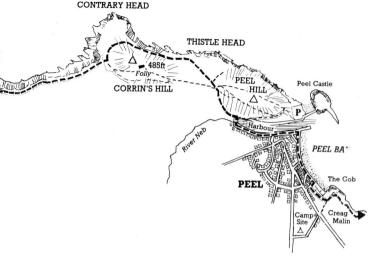

Follow the wide path upstream along the verdant ravine of Glen Maye. Cross an unusual bridge. If the water is high you may have to paddle. The song of the stream is now on your right. At the car park turn left. Signpost (w/m).

A gate on your right gives access to the site of the Mona Erin Water Wheel which was used to service a small lead mine in 1868. This is also the bottom entrance to Glen Maye, one of the Island's national glens, which contains a beautiful waterfall, well worth a visit.

At the signpost you will notice that our companion gull has caught two herrings. This marks the Bayr ny Skeddan, the 'Herring Road' footpath from Peel to Castletown.

The rising path crosses a stone stile and emerges from the trees to renew the seascape. Do not take the left fork. It leads down to the steps by the shelter in the bay. The path continues to rise and follows the cliff edge easily. Gradually gain height above a fine cliff, then as the path bends left do not be tempted into the field at a gap but keep ahead down the narrow path between the field and the cliff edge.

Stonechats and meadow pipits frequent the top of the cliff. If you listen for their chirping you will easily identify them as they are not so shy and continue their busy search of the gorse bushes scarcely heeding strangers.

The path now loses height and away in the distance to the south there is a last glimpse of the Calf of Man. Ahead Corrin's Hill and its Folly seem close at hand.

69

Niarbyl, the Tail of Rocks, from Cronk ny Arrey Laa

Turn right into a field by means of a stile, splash across or skirt round a boggy hollow as best you can. In about 100yds. regain the cliff edge again by means of another stile and carry on. A metal wicket gate is the next pause, soon followed by another and yet a third to reach the foot of Corrin's Hill. Signpost (w/m).

Turn left following the line of the wall. The path leaves the wall at a fin of rock to circle the hill on its seaward side. At a fork go where fancy leads you. Both paths join again in a short while to continue along the cliff edge.

The path is straight and wide and rising. You walk this sublime terrace as a visitor. The gulls which ride the air at eye level and preen on their soft balcony will lend it briefly while you pass by. Go through a wicket gate (w/m) and straight on to the col between Corrin's Hill and Peel Hill.

An alternative route taking you over Corrin's Hill is straightforward. From the signpost at the foot of the hill a prominent path leads directly to the tower and descends to the col on the other side. The tower was built in 1806 by Thomas Corrin as a memorial to his family. It is fifty feet high and the corners of the tower point to the four cardinal points of the compass. Corrin built the tower on the highest point of his land 500ft. above the sea. He, his wife and child are buried nearby.

Looking back along the coast from Contrary Head.

At the col two minor paths branch right towards Peel. The first is the official route which descends steeply to the road and bridge. It is a leg-scratcher. It is better to take your first view of Peel from the broad green track which rises over Peel Hill, so keep straight ahead as the broad green track swings away right and as you come over the crest of the hill prepare for the grand finale. Peel Castle and the town enfold the picturesque harbour where the River Neb quietly enters the sea. Here is a spot to linger in the sunset, but if time is short turn right along the gravel track to the river bridge (w/m). Cross over the river into Peel.

Oyster Catcher

PEEL

Tourist Information
Peel Town Commissioners, Derby Road. Tel: (84) 62341

Accommodation
Hotels, B&B
Moore, The Eaves, Derby Road, Peel. Tel: (0624) 842557
Conning, Glen Holme, Derby Road. Tel: (0624) 843683
Camp Site, Derby Road. Hot water, clothes wash and dry.

Public Transport
Bus runs from the Town Hall
Peel - Douglas, Ramsey, Port Erin, Castletown, Airport,
Glen Maye and Dalby for Niarbyl.

Services
Full range of shops. Early closing Thursday.

Places of Interest
Peel Castle; St. German's Cathedral; Viking Longship
Odin's Raven Museum, Mill Road - Open Easter-September, Sunday-Friday;
Kipper Factory.

On the descent of Peel Hill, the castle and town below

PEEL
to
KIRK MICHAEL

Distance: 7½ miles.   Maximum height reached 200ft.

This section of the Raad ny Foillan is completely different to anything that has gone before, yet is equally scenic, interesting and enjoyable. On leaving Peel the colour of the cliffs change to red sandstone. The profile of the inland hills are lower to the north, and the straight coastline ahead hints at the long miles along the beach to where Jurby Point melts into a purple haze. The coast is followed for just over a mile, then a short stretch on the road allows you to meet the old railway at the disused station of St. Germaine's Halt. The old track carries the Raad ny Foillan through cuttings, over bridges, along parts of the coast visited only by birds and butterflies as far as Glen Mooar. Here a descent is made down the beautiful glen with its lush woodland and cascading stream to the beach. High cliffs of conglomerate bound the sea and after a mile along the beach the first break in these is Glen Wyllin, where the footpath climbs up onto the railway again and into Kirk Michael.

7. PEEL to KIRK MICHAEL

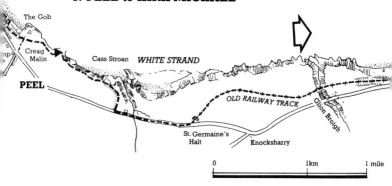

The Route

The town of Peel sits insignificantly alongside its proud castle and fascinating harbour. In the summer Viking longships ride at anchor, their fearsome prows nodding, disturbed by the wakes of their modern descendants.

From the river bridge waymark by a huge anchor, turn left and walk along the quayside. At the telephone box (w/m) turn right along the promenade. Turn right up Walpole Road (w/m) then take the path left. (Near the end of the promenade are the toilets. From there turn right immediately beyond the tennis courts and a flight of steps leads to the same path.) When the wall ends a signpost ahead on the right indicates the continuing footpath beyond the bowling greens. The red sandstone cliffs have replaced the Manx slate and the coast now shows a different, though equally beautiful facet.

Pass through the red gateway and past the foundations of an old building. This was the Peveril Internment Camp, used during World War II. Those detained were under the 18B clause allowing, 'any person suspected of enemy connections to be interned without trial'.

The paving ends at an iron wicket gate (w/m) and through this you emerge onto the cliff path.

This is the Craig Malin headland where the Manx forefathers kept watch for the approach of the dreaded Cullock-Mac-Cullock, a notorious Galloway chief. According to an old Manx song he would 'carry off all not too hot nor too heavy'.

Pass by a deep dyke then through a wicket gate. The path is easy and your eyes will be continually drawn down the plunging cliffs to the sea. Do not become too distracted; bend right at Cass Struan.

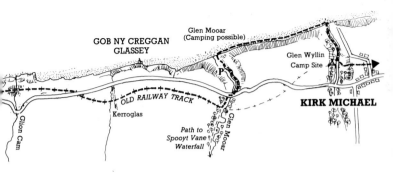

Note: Another little hiccough with the map. It is necessary to turn the Isle of Man Public Rights of Way and Leisure Map over for this section. The coast path of the Raad ny Foillan is marked in red to Cass Struan then swings off the map to join the familiar blue on the road.

Go through a wicket gate and descend the steps. Signpost (w/m). You can do a sneaky by-pass round the next wicket gate and carry on until you join the road. The route is now marked in blue again on the map. Turn left following the road north east for just less than a mile until you arrive at the spot where an old railway track crosses the road at St. Germaine's Halt. Signpost (w/m).

The railway, closed in 1968, ran a circuitous route from Douglas to Ramsey. It followed the valleys of the Rivers Dhoo, Greeba and Neb westward as far as St. Johns. Here a branch line continued along the Neb valley to Peel and the Ramsey line pushed north-west to the coast. At Kirk Michael it turned inland again and made its way east passing through Ballough and Sulby thence following the Sulby River to Ramsey. Our way follows the route of the old line for a while, the silent cuttings and embankments offering an undisturbed haven to a variety of wild life. The small and the beautiful; birds, butterflies and flowers. The large and formidable; in the shape of nomadic bulls.

I was enjoying the tranquility of this old railway. My eyes were roving the track for flowers and I failed to notice the pride of the herd leading his followers to pastures new. I did not contest my right of way but almost literally flew down the embankment, over the ditch and fence to the safety of the field where I trespassed unashamed. My slightly less agile companion soon joined me muttering about the way of the gull being suddenly transformed to the way of the bull. Beware!

Crossing the embankment at Glion Cam

The green mound in the field on your left is an ancient earthwork, the site of a Pictish round house. Being out of sight and sound of the sea you may have forgotten that you are the way of the gull - on this track you are more aware of the hills to the east than the sea. From the south-east *Slieau Ruy 1570ft., Coldon 1599ft., Sartfell 1490ft., Slieau Freoghane 1601ft., and Slieau Curn 1153ft.* just north of Kirk Michael, form an impressive backcloth -but suddenly you can gaze ahead onto wide beaches and the view reminds you that you are still on the *Raad ny Foillan.*

The square tower at Kirk Michael is now in view.

At the next lane the railway bridge has gone. Go down the steps on the left (w/m), cross the lane, then regain the railway. A succession of two gates, a lane, a little footbridge and another gate follow. Now prepare for a surprise. The old viaduct over Glen Mooar has gone and its guardian rail brings you to a sudden halt. The void is dramatic. A lone pier stands proud accusing the march of progress. Say 'au revoir' to the railway and turn left down a steep path into Glen Mooar. Signpost (w/m).

Excursion to Spooyt Vane

Spooyt Vane is a pretty three-tiered waterfall. At the base of the old viaduct turn right up the glen. A cosseted path climbs gently to the site of Patrick's Chapel (8th-10th century), then continues to climb to the head of the

Remains of the old viaduct at Glen Mooar

waterfall. A series of steps on the left lead down the steep valley-side allowing you to view the full length of the waterfall.

In the shady glen turn left downstream to meet the road. Cross the road (w/m) and continue down by the hurrying stream. Cross over the footbridge by a ford and in a few minutes you will reach the beach, where there are possibilities of camping for the backpacker. At Glen Mooar the facilities are simple. A tiny portaloo - toilet and handwash basin - is in the car park. The limited camping is on the south of the stream bordering the beach. A delightful spot where you can be lulled to sleep by the song of the sea and woken by the cry of the gull.

At the beach turn right (w/m) and walk along the beach for a mile to Glen Wyllin. The sand is firm and passable at high tide but a word of caution: From Douglas the sea has been your friendly neighbour. Its tides and moods regarding you from a safe distance. At Glen Mooar you step into its front garden. Be aware of the state of the tide and remember that a driving wind and a high tide may change circumstances. The cliffs are composed of glacial drift and are very unstable so do not rely on them as an escape route. Local people use the beach daily and one gentleman said that he had only been stopped by the tide once. To quote the local workmen from The Department of Forests, Mines and Lands Board, 'except when a really high spring

77

tide is backed by a storm wind you can always walk along the beach'.
See section on tides, page 15.

No need to watch your feet. Just walk and enjoy the blend of sounds
and smells, shades and textures. This short stretch of beach is a small
sample of things to come.

The next gap in the cliffs is Glen Wyllin. Turn right up the glen
(w/m) towards Kirk Michael.

Glen Wyllin camp site is a large camp site with full facilities, open
May-mid September.

At the camp site the remains of the railway viaduct stand in the
valley. Cross the bridge (w/m) and climb the steps under the topless
viaduct to gain the old railway again. Follow the railway northward
until you come to the vestige of the old level crossing on the outskirts
of Kirk Michael.

The way takes to the beach at Glen Mooar

KIRK MICHAEL

Tourist Information
Kirk Michael Village Commissioners, Tel: (878) 202

Accommodation
Farmhouse B&B
Kneal, Ballachristory Farm, Jurby East. Tel: (897) 646
Camp Sites - Glen Wyllin, June-September
Hot/cold showers, clothes wash & Dry, small shop
Glen Mooar - toilets & handwash basin, cold water. Open all year.

Public Transport
Bus - Peel, Ramsey

Services
Post Office, general store, butcher, garage (at N end of village sells paraffin), doctor, bank, café (summer).

Places of Interest
Jurby Church; Spooyt Vane waterfall; Glen Mooar;
Bishop's Court, a 14th century mansion and its glen;
Ayres Nature Reserve Visitor Centre.

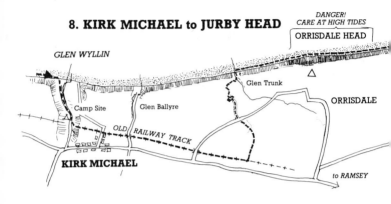

8. KIRK MICHAEL to JURBY HEAD

DANGER!
CARE AT HIGH TIDES

ORRISDALE HEAD

GLEN WYLLIN

Glen Trunk

ORRISDALE

Camp Site   Glen Ballyre

OLD RAILWAY TRACK

KIRK MICHAEL

to RAMSEY

KIRK MICHAEL
to
POINT OF AYRE

Distance: 15 miles - sea level

A short stretch on the old railway gives easy walking through pleasant rural landscape. Then, back to the beach and straight on past impressive sea cliffs. The coastline is not as straight as it appears on the map. The sand is firm yet when the cliffs recede the heathland path is a welcome change. Check the state of the tide and wind speed. If the tide is approaching high watermark on a spring tide with a westerly gale-force wind, postpone your passage until the tide is on the ebb. The Jurby section of beach has a remote, exposed atmosphere. Jurby church offers unique historical interest. The change from glacial drift to sands and gravels gives a geologically young, gently undulating environment on which the Ayres Nature Reserve is situated. The Point of Ayre Lighthouse forms a worthy finish to this most northerly part of the Isle of Man. If you enjoy the company of seabirds, seals and plants you will find this section of the Raad ny Foillan outstanding.

80

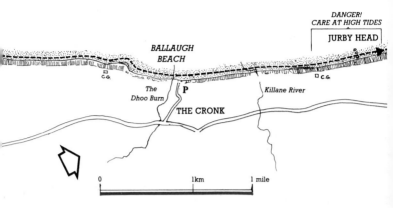

The Route

Leave Kirk Michael by the long-gone level crossing and go through the fire station yard, still on the track of the old railway. The tower of Kirk Michael church is prominent on the right, with Slieau Curn 1184ft., Slieau Dhoo 1417ft. and Slieau Freoghane 1601ft., forming the horizon to the east. Keep on the railway over two footbridges, under two stone bridges, through a cutting then look out for a gate on the left where a path crosses the line (w/m). Here the Raad ny Foillan says goodbye to the railway track. Turn left along an embanked footpath and through a wicket gate into a field. Follow the edge of the field to a gate and lane, signpost (w/m). Cross the lane to a bridle track, signpost (w/m).

From the bridle track look north over the valley of Glen Trunk. A narrow road, known as the 'old trunk road' leads from the beach to an old limekiln. Limestone was brought by boat from the quarries at Scarlett Point and carried up to the kiln where it was made into lime for agricultural use. The limestone was packed into the kiln with wood or charcoal, in alternate layers. It was then fired with a controlled air supply. This gave quicklime which was slaked with water then was ready to use for agriculture.

Wind round the back of Ballarhenny Beg and go down, alongside a wall. Look how the wall is made in the traditional way, from earth set with pebbles and topped with turf. Descend into the deep cut, little

81

Walking the beach, Peel Hill in the far distance

valley of Glen Trunk. Cross the stream, climb up to the signpost (w/m) then down left to the beach. Turn right, check the time and tide, then set the automatic pilot north-north-east for the Point of Ayre.

Although the map indicates a 13½ mile trudge along the sand the reality is far better than the anticipation. The cliffs of Orrisdale Head soon pass by. They have been sculptured by water from glacial drift, with sand avalanches resembling giant egg-timers counting the tides. An old coastguard beacon in the distance grows nearer as the cliffs lower. Along this stretch of beach I had the companionship of a friendly seal. Swimming a few yards from the breakers it followed my progress as far as the Ballaugh beach car park. Ballaugh - (1½ miles from the Raad ny Foillan), supermarket.

In 1697 at Ballaugh 'there was a remarkable wreck in this parish of a small vessel loaded with brandy, the first ever known on this island'. The taste for the spirit must have been rapidly acquired for in 1698 Bishop Wilson arrived to find, 'a rising tide of imported spirits'. He tried his best to turn back the tide, but like King Canute, had no success. The merchants of the Island had set up a very lucrative business, importing good liquor at a ridiculously low rate of Manx duty. It was all legal and above board. They then transferred it to smugglers who passed it on at a profit. Ballaugh was one of the favourite beaches for the smugglers.

A gap allows the Dhoo Burn to enter the sea (w/m). On the north side of the car park is a sheltered picnic spot but no camping is allowed. The nearby hamlet of Cronk has a telephone but no shops. Continue along the beach to the gap in the cliffs where the Killane River enters the sea.

This is the nearest point south from which Jurby church can be visited, Sartfield being the next access path from the beach, three miles to the north. Jurby church is a prominent landmark.

In the porch of Jurby church is housed a fine collection of Manx crosses of 6th to 12th century origin. Casts of these are now exhibited in the Manx Museum. Two of the master sculptors working from 990-1050AD were Gaut Bjornson, who was born on the Isle of Coll, Scotland, and Thorbjorn. It was Thorbjorn who carved the Sigurd crosses. The Sigurd slab tells of the slaying of Fafnir the dragon and other stories, now immortalised in legend, stone and the well-known operas of Wagner. Plaques on the wall explain the crosses to the visitor and help to identify the figures. These crosses are unique but the collection at Maughold is much more accessible for the Raad ny Foillan walker. (see page 97.)

Grey Atlantic seal

After Jurby Point the cliffs rise in weird shaped clay caverns and canyons. Passage along the beach should be possible throughout the year but there are always exceptions. Organise your passage of this section on an ebbing tide if you are in any doubt of the wave size and wind strength. The sheer cliffs are unstable and attempts to escape that way are dangerous.

The Jurby airstrip is unused now, but when the original concrete was being laid a burial mound was discovered. This was hurriedly opened. It was found to have items of great interest, so it was carefully re-covered. After the war it was excavated and found to be the grave of a Scandinavian settler of great importance buried with his sword, shield and ornaments.

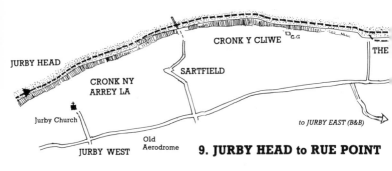

9. JURBY HEAD to RUE POINT

As the sand stretches on and on a few jolly songs and jaunty tales would not go amiss. The area through which you are now passing is rich in history and legend.

Let us contemplate an old Manx Saw:

> *'When a man wants a wife, he wants but a wife,*
> *But when he has a wife he wants a great deal.'*

A pipeline entering the sea indicates that you are level with Sartfield. The cliffs lower and marram grass consolidates the land from the sea. As the coastline veers an old coastguard station comes into view. Look for a signpost and (w/m) where a public footpath leads to the road. Another (w/m) at The Perk and a change of activity, it is possible to walk on a grassy shelf. Jump the stream at the outlet of the Lhen Trench, then back to the beach walking. Just round the headland with its coastguard hat and accompanying pill box is a (w/m) and a gap in the dunes which leads to the raised beach and the Blue Point car park. Alongside the car park is a clay pigeon shooting range. Do not enter if the white flag is flying.

Continue on the path between the wall-fence and the edge of the dunes. Here it is easier walking along the turf. This is a welcome change as the beach has become soft and pebbly. Duck under an old fence and carry on ahead. The pharos you have awaited with anticipation since Spanish Head now comes into view. The sight of the Point of Ayre Lighthouse puts the spring back into your feet.

Go through a gap in the fence towards the beach. Take your choice between the beach, a diminishing path threading its way through the marram grass, or continue with easier walking on the heath.

x

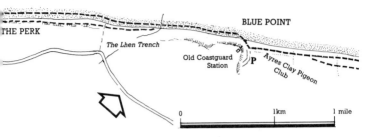

Marram grass was pulled by hand in large quantities and used as thatching in the north of the Island. Today its chief use is to bind the mobile sand with its matted roots and allows the clumps of sea holly to grow. Your feet testify that it is doing its duty.

Cross the access lane at Rue Point (w/m).

Wrecks have made some strange contributions to Man, but the strangest must have come with the schooner Hooton in 1805. She sailed from White-haven on the Cumbrian coast and was wrecked on Rue Point. Amongst the passengers' luggage was a box containing several hedgehogs, a species

Ballaugh Beach and Jurby Head

10. BLUE POINT to POINT OF AYRE

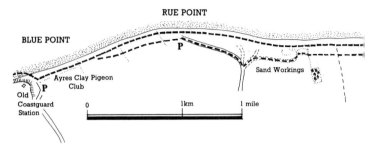

previously unknown to the Island. The rescued animals were distributed as pets amongst the local residents and have bred so prolifically that they are common throughout the Island.

From Rue Point it is easiest to walk on the heath which lies just behind the sand dunes. For a while a narrow concrete road makes easy going, until it swings away to the right. You have now entered the Ayres area of public ramblage. On the left are sand diggings, the dunes and the beach. Take to the beach once more or continue on the

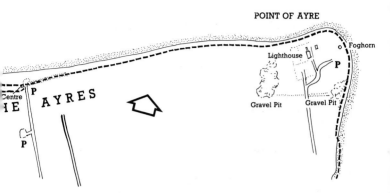

rough track on the heath. A slight path parallel to the shore begins to thread its way through the dunes. If you want to examine the flora of this special environment this is the place to do so.

The Manx Nature Conservation Trust have set up a Nature Trail and Visitors' Centre. The area is one favoured by rare plants and birds in need of conservation. It is composed of different environments, varying with the measure of consolidation achieved by the sands and gravels. There are examples of shingle, dune, heath and raised beach. In winter the water-table is very high and for short periods, parts stand flooded by fresh water. Information boards tell you of the wild life to be seen in the area.

When opposite a stand of pine trees in the middle distance to your right, the Ayres plantation, a good path runs in a trough parallel to the beach and makes faster and more interesting going.

The next landmark is a signpost - Public footpath to Allaggarrett. The roof of the Ayres Visitors' Centre is in sight. A National Trust sign and information board show that you have entered the reserve. **Note:** the centre has moved from its position at the end of a paved footpath to the position marked 'P' (parking) on both maps. About 500yds. along the road inland is another National Trust car park. This is surrounded by trees and bushes and offers a pleasant sheltered spot for a quiet meal or perhaps a sheltered bivouac.

Leave the Ayres Visitors' Centre by the paved footpath 50yds. inland from a point opposite the building N.E. and continue along a well trodden path to the lighthouse.

Curlews, oystercatchers, ringed plovers, little terns, and common terns like to nest in these marram dunes and a notice begs walkers to watch their step and not to linger, so as not to disturb the nesting birds. Remember that

87

Point of Ayre Lighthouse

the longer you take to pass, the longer the eggs or young are unprotected and exr. sed to the cold or predators. The black-headed gulls like to nest in a disuse 1 gravel pit next to the refuse dump.

ine Point of Ayre Lighthouse is open to the public but not every day. The keeper has to sleep and a notice-board outside will tell you if it is your lucky day.

The Isle of Man Lights are controlled by the Northern Lights Board of Scotland, not by Trinity House. The Point of Ayre Lighthouse was built between 1815 and 1818 by Robert Louis Stevenson's grandfather.

Toilets near the lighthouse are open all year.

There is a tap in the gents but in 1987 the top was missing (a small spanner would be useful). No tap in the ladies.

Arctic Tern

POINT of AYRE
to RAMSEY

Distance: 7 miles - sea level.

On leaving the Point of Ayre the old salt and later gravel workings are rather unpleasant. The soft pebbly beach with the prevailing wind in my face gave me a feeling of anticlimax. It only lasted a hundred yards.

The fine quality of the Raad ny Foillan is quickly rekindled. As you travel south the cliffs rise and, as the Glacial Drift Boulder Clay is met, become more spectacular.

Check the tide and wind speed.

The scene ahead gains interest as the hills, North Barrule, Slieau Managh and Snaefell grow nearer. Ramsey Bay sweeps east to terminate in Maughold Head. This sets you looking forward with anticipation, to enjoying its footpath. The walking, all on the beach, becomes firmer and easier. Ramsey is reached perhaps more quickly than anticipated.

The Route

Being at sea level the viewpoint is not the best, yet on a clear day the Galloway hills seem very close (Burrow Head, Galloway, 18 miles). I found that the anticipation was in fact better than the realisation on the day I passed by, for it was misty and the lighthouse was closed.

In the 19th century borings were made at the Point of Ayre in the search for coal. They were unsuccessful as far as the coal was concerned, but salt was found at a depth of 600ft in the Triassic marls below the glacial drift. Water was pumped down and brine brought to the surface which was piped to the salt works at Ramsey. This worked well for a while, but by 1956 salt obtained in this way proved uneconomical and the workings were abandoned.

Pass the fog horn and turn south (w/m). Go through the derelict workings. (Gravel was being taken for road building, but this gave rise to erosion further south along the coast, and had to be stopped.) Away to the south the distant peak of North Barrule above Ramsey beckons. Follow the edge of the shingle looking out for the remains of the concrete pier.

11. POINT OF AYRE to RAMSEY

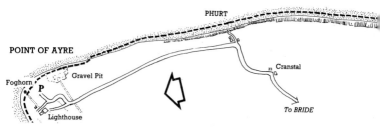

A short way south of the pier metal rods and pieces of concrete can sometimes be seen. These are the remains of a concrete ship. The 'Burscough' was built in Preston, Lancashire and was launched in 1921. She was a motor vessel of 229 tons and as steel was in short supply she was built of reinforced concrete. Her short life was dogged with trouble. She made a successful voyage to Kingstown with a cargo of coal then the difficulties started. Her engines failed her and she had to be towed back to Preston from Douglas. In 1924 her fittings were removed and the hulk towed to the Point of Ayre. It was sunk to form part of the jetty.

The shingle is soft to walk on and in places it is possible to get better footing on the field edge. Pass by a tin hut and launching ramp where the hook of an old anchor lies half buried in the sand.

After passing the cottages of Phert (port) low cliffs begin to develop as the blown sands and gravels give way to the red conglomerates once more. The beach gravel gradually gives way to strips of sand and pebbles making the walking firmer. Looking onward Maughold Head beyond Ramsey forms the southern side of Ramsey Bay on the horizon.

Before going further check the state of the tide. There is little room for walking between the waves and the cliff at high tide. Take care when approaching the foot of the cliffs, as the cliffs are muddy, waterlogged and highly unstable, sending down fine granite boulders of Scottish origin from time to time.

From the beach Shellag Point stands out as a definite feature although the coast appears straight on the map. The first major break in the cliffs as you progress beyond Shellag Point shows that you have reached Kionlough. Steps and a(w/m) with a signpost *Dog Mills* point to the main road access. Carry on along the sand until you come to the end of the Ramsey promenade.

There are two local explanations of this strange name. The first tells of a dog in a trundle wheel, used to raise water in times of drought. The second

90

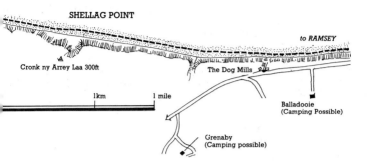

SHELLAG POINT

to RAMSEY

Cronk ny Arrey Laa 300ft

The Dog Mills

1km 1 mile

Balladooie
(Camping Possible)

Grenaby
(Camping possible)

speaks of the old flour mill, its stones making the noise of a whining dog.

If you have a streak of tuareg in you, you can carry on along the sand as far as the harbour. But if you have spent enough time in low gear, empty your boots, change up and stride out firmly along the promenade into Ramsey. At the harbour continue to follow the road round to the right. There is a water tap on a grey brick wall to the left just round the bend. Turn left over the bridge between the inner and outer harbours (w/m).

Below Shellag Point

Ramsey

RAMSEY

Tourist Information
Ramsey Town Commissioners, Town Hall, Bowring Road, Ramsey.
Tel: (0624) 812228

Accommodation
Hotels, B&B
The camp site is now closed.
Camping & B&B - Balladoole Farm. Tel: Ramsey 812240
Bradley, The Rhenwee Cottage, Kirk Andreas. Tel: 880250/ 880513
Cook, Field Head, Glen Mana, Maughold. Tel: Laxey 861133
Gaskell, Whitestones,Cardle Vooar Farm. Maughold. Tel: 813824
Hopkins, Riverside, Maughold. Tel: Laxey 861677
Wartons, Mountain View, Kirk Andreas.

Public Transport
BUS starts from the Depot, Queen's Pier Road.
Ramsey to Douglas via Laxey, Onchan.
Douglas via Sulby, Wild Life Park, Kirk Michael, Peel.
Jurby via St. Jude's.   Point of Ayre via Bride.   Maughold.
ELECTRIC TRAIN April to October. Station Albert Street.
Ramsey to Douglas via Ballajora, Ballaglass, Dhoon, Laxey, Garwick,
Groudle.

Services
Full range of shops. Early closing - Wednesday
Coastguard Headquarters. Tel: Ramsey 813255
Heated Swimming Pool, with café. Hospital.

Places of Interest
Rural Life Museum; Wild Life Park Ballaugh; Mooragh Park; Celtic Music
& Dance festival, Mid July.

RAMSEY
to LAXEY

Distance: 13 miles.   Maximum height reached 650ft.

Throughout this section an interesting mixture of cliff and glen, meadow and lane are met. The sudden change from Glacial Drift to the Manx Slates is clearly seen in the sheer rugged cliffs of the coast, the change of vegetation and gradient of the Raad ny Foillan.

The sections of road walking are mainly on quiet lanes with interesting hedgerows, or wide views.

The highlights of the section must be the traverse of Maughold Head and the descent of lovely Glen Cornaa.

An excursion into Dhoon Glen, one of the most beautiful on the Island would not go unrewarded.

The walking is rocky in places and demands care. The footpath makes and descends 1,200ft. in three visits to sea level from the coastal plateau. The gradients are so easy that they mostly pass unnoticed.

The footpath passes by Maughold Church and the Ballafoyle Cairn, sites of prime historical interest.

The Route
At the harbour bridge (w/m) turn left towards the sea and follow the side of the harbour, bending left at the market place along the East Quay.

I cannot resist the fascination of a working harbour. Boats of all shapes and sizes with the nautical flavour reflected in the buildings - The Isle of Man Steam Packet Company, the Harbourmaster's office, complete with barometer and tide timetable. Useful if you are doing the Raad ny Foillan anticlockwise.

Turn right along the south promenade to the Queen's Pier (w/m). (The blue routemark on the map is wrong for the next 750yds.)
At low tide go down the steps and along the beach until twin arches and a stream are seen. Go through the first arch and up the Ballure Glen by the path alongside its stream. Cross over the footbridge. A zig-zag path climbs up through pleasant gardens to a railway crossing.

The Manx Electric Railway runs from Ramsey to Douglas. From May to September there are five trains daily in each direction and though the

12. RAMSEY to PORT MOOAR

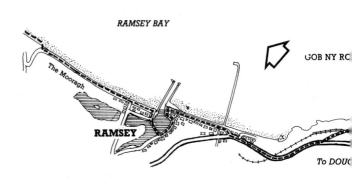

rolling stock with its leather seats and tassels may look quaint, there is nothing sedate about the speed with which it hurtles round the corners and darts in and out of the cuttings. You will cross its track many times before you reach Douglas so take care. Before you cross the line look and listen.

Cross the railway line to the main road (w/m).

At high tide from the Queen's pier keep on the road until in 100yds. it joins the main road to Laxey. Continue towards Laxey until you cross over the railway bridge and find the waymark at the path junction.

Keep along the main road for 600yds. then fork left towards Maughold (w/m). Cross a railway bridge and look for a waymark and signpost, Port e Vullen, on your left. Turn left (Manx National Trust: Gob ny Rona) and take the green path ahead to a small car park.

This must be a spot loved by the local photographers for you can see the coastline stretching away north to the Point of Ayre, the lighthouse a tiny white pin, cushioned on the horizon.

Follow the sea wall round the headland. A fine view of Maughold Head can be enjoyed until steps lead down to the beach at Port e Vullen. Signpost.

The outcropping rocks on the beach have been eroded into strange and flowing shapes, the exposed strata in its pristine colours rivalling the mobile beauty of the surf in stone.

A concrete ramp from the beach will lead you to the road. A cameo of Queen Victoria is mounted on the gable of a house to the right. At

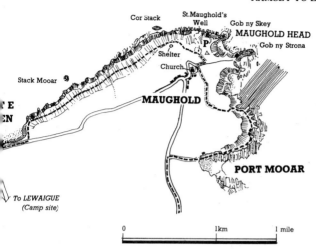

the road is a signpost (w/m). Turn left up the road for 300yds. keeping on the same side of the road.

Leave the road at a wicket gate, (w/m) signpost: Maughold Brooghs, and another wicket gate takes you back into the wild.

A herd of Loaghtan, the four-horned Manx sheep, live here so you are certain to get a chance to admire them. The male is a small but handsome fellow with four re-curved horns and a coffee coloured fleece. The female has two shorter horns. They are almost goat-like in their agility and suit well their rugged surroundings. I recently saw another fine herd of Loaghtan in Shropshire but their almost luxurious field did not complement them like the rugged coast of their isle.

At the start of the path a sign warns you of rough walking to come. Do not be alarmed, the path with Stack Mooar below, is narrow but easy to follow. Two fine pine trees by a wicket gate sing in the wind as the path begins to climb. Look back where Albert Tower appears in silhouette.

The tower commemorates the spot from which the Prince Consort viewed Ramsey in 1847. The royal party were to have landed at Douglas but, as often happens when royalty approach the Isle of Man, the ancient necromancer and King Manannan McLir, threw a curtain of mist around Douglas and Queen Victoria and Prince Albert were diverted to Ramsey. By the time the reception committee had reached Ramsey the Prince had climbed the hill, admired the view, and gone.

Queen Elizabeth II and Prince Philip visited the Island on a beautiful sunny day in 1955. As the royal yacht approached the Island a thick fog settled. As the Queen sailed away in the evening the fog evaporated to leave clear skies. Draw your own conclusions.

Look ahead where Cor Stack down at sea level helps you appreciate the invisible 300ft. contour you are crossing and as you continue to gain height North Barrule comes into view, but do not stop here because shelter and viewpoint indicator soon comes along, complete with seat.

The footpath now begins to descend to a wall corner. Keep by the wall then pass through a gap in the cross wall. Continue to lose height to a Manx National Trust sign. Go through the gap in a cross wall into a grassy hollow. A path branching left down the cliff leads to St. Maughold's Well and Maughold Head.

On the cliffs below is a large kittiwake colony. It is a popular spot with four types of auks breeding here.

A wicket gate ahead gives access to the car park (w/m) signpost.

The car park provides a sheltered picnic or bivouac spot.

Go down the lane leading from the car park. Turn right along the minor road, then left at the graveyard.

To reach the toilets and tap in Maughold village, go through the churchyard to the village green. The toilets are up a narrow lane on the right.

Maughold may be a tiny community but it has a huge hoard of history within sight of its pretty village green.

Maughold Head is the furthest point east on the Isle of Man. Its lighthouse is not visible at the moment from the Raad ny Foillan, but it will come into view presently. Cliffs of Barrule Slates and quartz-veined grits fall sheer to the sea, where they are washed by tidal currents which tend to push north-east up the Irish Sea. These currents brought Maughold its name and the Island one of its most revered ancestors.

Tradition tells of Machud or MacCuill, a pagan robber, whom St. Patrick converted to Christianity. As a penance for his former sins St. Patrick ordered that Machud should be chained, set adrift in a wicker coracle and left to the mercy of God. The coracle drifted out to sea and was carried by the tide to the headland where it was dashed to pieces on its jagged rocks. Two men chanced to be at hand. They pulled Machud from the breakers and as he touched land his chains fell off and he was freed. They climbed the cliffs and when Machud reached the grassy slopes he fell on his knees and gave thanks for his deliverance. On that spot a spring gushed from the ground. St. Maughold's Well, it was named. Machud spent the rest of his life in the service of God. Helped by the local people he

96

The old Market Cross, in Maughold Churchyard

built a little church on the headland and travelled around preaching and teaching. He became bishop to the Island and was known at St. Machud or St. Maughold. He died in 553, so it is said, and was buried in his church-yard.

Along the side wall of the churchyard at Maughold a shelter has been made for the collection of ancient stones. Forty-four pieces, crosses and slabs dating from the 6th-12th centuries are displayed. The Scandinavian crosses continue the story of Sigurd.

One other cross, the Maughold Cross, is the village cross. It has been moved from the village green into the churchyard. Its special interest is the carved shield with the three legs of Man. This is one of the oldest represent-

97

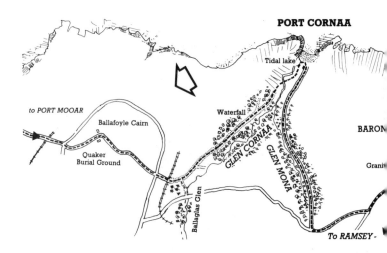

ations of the well-known national emblem, the other being on the Manx sword of state. This sword was carried into battle by Olaf Godredson when he fought the Moors of Spain in 1230. The same sword is carried by the Governor in the procession on Tynwald Day.

The church itself is of great interest. The porch has a Celtic arch springing from a capitol with a human face on the front and beasts at each side. There is more 10th century work to be seen. The font is very large and must have been meant for total immersion. In the churchyard which was once fortified by a wall and ditch, are the ruins of two ancient keeills. I would not have expected this esteemed spot to be connected with pirate's treasure but it is. A gold coin was found in the church wall. It was of the date of Louis le Debonnaire, son of Charlemagne. It is presumed to be part of a Scandinavian pirate hoard and is now in the Manx Museum.

From the signpost (w/m) at the corner of Maughold churchyard turn left down the green lane, through a gate on a right bend and continue past a signpost on a left bend. The lane ends at a stone stile. Straight on to a high ladder stile. The extra few feet in height gained by the stile is useful. From the top of the stile the Maughold Head Lighthouse can be seen on the left. Turn left and zig-zag down to the tiny cove of Dhyrnane. Our path circles the cove and climbs worn steps to traverse above the rocks.

Just beyond the cove a flat-topped rock platform protrudes into the sea from path level.

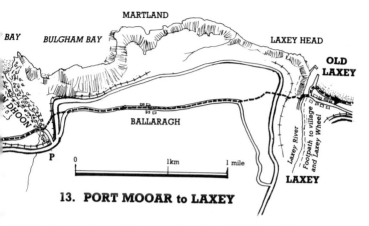

13. **PORT MOOAR to LAXEY**

This is the place from which to examine Maughold Head. I first visited these cliffs some years ago as a rock climber. A natural rock arch and two pinnacles, the Twin Cletts, provide entertaining sport, whilst the grey atlantic seals form an inquisitive audience.

Maughold Head

Walk on along the grass path into the larger bay of Port Mooar. Take to the beach to reach the car park.

Here the Raad ny Foillan has to leave the coast for a while as there is no public right of way at the time of writing, but 'it's an ill wind' and the change of scene more than compensates.

Make your way up the narrow road to a minor road signpost (w/m). turn left and go along the road for ¾ mile crossing over the railway bridge to Ballajora.

At the crossroads go almost straight across (w/m) and up the hill. On the crest is a grove of pines.

The Ballafoyle Cairn, the remains of a neolithic burial site can be seen on the left of the lane, together with the site of an ancient Keeill. On the right is the Quaker's burial ground Rhullick-ny-Quakeryn. The Quakers were severely persecuted by Bishop Barrow (1663) and many died in dreadful circumstances.

The height from this lane presents a fine panorama of the central highlands. The wooded line of upper Glen Cornaa draws the eye to Snaefell with North Barrule to its right and Slieau Duyr on its left.

Cross a wider road (w/m), and descend into the deep valley of Glen Cornaa. Here you meet the railway again and do not forget that it is very much alive on this side of the Island. Go straight down the lane,

The Ballafoyle Cairn

Glen Cornaa

signpost (w/m), along the glenside. A bridle track veers right. Keep straight on, over a stile, signpost, and through a beautiful beech grove. Ignore a track forking left and keep straight on. Waterfalls, pools in the river and an ideal picnic spot invite you to stay a while. Carry on through a gate.

On the right an old concrete ruin can be seen amongst the trees. It never grew beyond a foundation as its purpose was nipped in the bud. A Swedish gentleman began the building in the middle of the last century. He intended to manufacture Belite (gunpowder) and export it from a tiny quay which he built in the bay. However, the Manx Government discovered his intentions and rapidly brought his activities to a halt, leaving nature to disguise the stark remains.

Cross over the bridge to gain access to the beach. The turf between the bridge and the beach floods at high tide, signpost (w/m).

Leave Port Cornaa by the road up Glen Mona.

Walk up the Glen road and carry straight on where a narrow road joins at a ford (1¼ miles). At the T-junction turn left (w/m), then cross the railway to the main road (w/m). Turn left and left again in 150yds. ignoring the lane, also on the left, to Dhoon Quarry.

The Dhoon granite has been quarried for many years. It is grey mottled granite and was exported as granite setts for the roads of Lancashire and Yorkshire. It is used as road metal on Man today and can be seen in local buildings.

The Electric Railway

Go straight on over the next level crossing. A confirmation waymark is welcome along the next ¾ mile stretch of road.

The valley to seaward is Dhoon Glen leading to Dhoon Bay, a renowned beauty spot and well worth a visit. There is a waterfall which falls 160ft. in 3 leaps; some interesting old mine workings where the stone housing for a 50ft waterwheel remains; and a beach where the Dhoon flags form attractive rock pools. If you follow the path by the stream down to the beach a return to the Raad ny Foillan can be made by crossing the stream on the beach, a path soon turns right and climbs steeply to a viewpoint. A good place for bird watching. Fulmar petrels nest on the cliffs. Ignore a small path on the right, keep on the main path along the cliff top which soon swings sharp right inland overlooking the glen. At a stile onto the minor road you are back on the Raad ny Foillan. The circuit down Dhoon Glen is about 3 miles and takes 1¾ hours, that is if you are not tempted to have a paddle.

A ladder stile over a wall is the next thing to look for. Signpost Ballaragh Road (w/m). Go over the stile and through the gate. Follow the fence wall to the far field corner. Four steps and a stile lead into bracken. You are not lost; follow the wall to another stile and stone steps to cross the railway line. Cross the main road. Mount a stile into the field. Signpost.

Scan the horizon ahead and uphill for a Manx National Trust sign.

Make for this and you will find a signpost and waymark where you meet, and turn left on the next minor road.

Having gained some height there is a splendid view over Dhoon Glen and the coast to the north-east, Slieau Lhean and Slieau Duyr to the north-west. From here you can study your progress south.

Keep along this minor road for 1¼ miles. Ignore a signpost to 'coast road' (w/m) and 'public footpath to main road' (w/m). The waymarks confirm that the road is still the way. Where the hill steepens look for a (w/m) on the left as the road bends right. Leave the road and go down a hedged bridle track. Cross the main road, waymarks to right. The valley of the Laxey river is before you. Take the descending footpath and cross the railway. The footpath narrows and steepens then joins an alpine-style road. Take no notice of the signpost on the left and you will arrive in a minute at the Laxey harbour bridge.

The Laxey Wheel and the Mines Trail.   103

Anchor at Old Laxey

LAXEY

Tourist Information
Laxey Village Commissioners, New Road, Laxey.
Tel: 861241

Accommodation
Hotels, B&B
Camp site with full facilities, Quarry Road, Laxey

Public Transport
Bus to Douglas and Ramsey
Electric Train to Douglas and Ramsey
Mountain Railway to Snaefell summit.

Services
Shops. Early closing Thursday

Places of Interest
The Laxey Wheel and Mines Trail; St. George's Woollen Mills (sells woollen socks).

LAXEY
to
DOUGLAS

Distance: 9½ miles.   Maximum height reached: 350ft.

The Raad ny Foillan now passes through the most densely populated part of the Island.

This section contains some stretches on the main road which the authorities know are unsatisfactory and are doing their best to improve.

Having said this, let me quote the words of a fellow walker 'I walked from Douglas to Laxey along the Raad ny Foillan and much enjoyed it - to my surprise'.

The path visits the peaceful havens of Garwick Bay and Port Groudle. The lanes and paths over Clay Head have extensive views. The descent of the Onchan Head Moor is a sudden surprise, and almost last but not least, the generosity of the local residents in allowing the footpath to go through their gardens is princely. The final stroll along the Douglas promenade is a satisfying completion of the circuit.

The Route
The estuary of the River Laxey forms the picturesque harbour. The bridge is the place to leave the Raad ny Foillan if you want to visit the famous Laxey Wheel; stay or shop in the village (there is a grocer's shop 100yds. across the bridge); visit the woollen mill or camp for the night.

Cross the river bridge and turn left (w/m), along the picturesque harbour side to the sea wall.

Laxey means salmon in Manx. Salmon still run up the Dhoo, Glass, Santon and Sulby rivers, and the Board of Agriculture and Fisheries have a breeding station at Maughold from which they restock the rivers. A fisherman I spoke to didn't mention salmon. His main interest was his catch of scallops and queenies which he took to the seafood factory at Port St. Mary.

The harbour is built Cornish style. The inner harbour dries out at low tide and is sheltered by Laxey Head and a sturdy stone pier. There are public

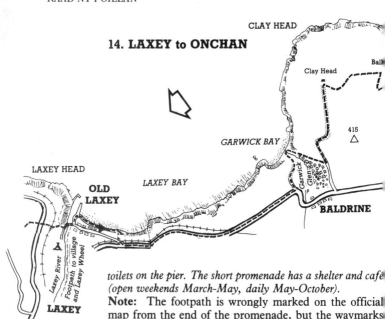

14. LAXEY to ONCHAN

CLAY HEAD

Clay Head

Ball

GARWICK BAY

415 △

LAXEY HEAD

OLD LAXEY

LAXEY BAY

Garwick Glen

BALDRINE

Laxey River

Footpath to village and Laxey Wheel

LAXEY

toilets on the pier. The short promenade has a shelter and café *(open weekends March-May, daily May-October).*

Note: The footpath is wrongly marked on the official map from the end of the promenade, but the waymarks have been adjusted and are correct.

The footpath is shown on the map as following the coast as far as the headland of Gob y Rheyin. At the end of the promenade the beach gives way to rocks, washed at high tide, seaweed covered at low tide. It is feasible to scramble a few hundred yards to an old mine trial, possibly serviced by a long absent walkway. A deep zawn cuts into the overhanging cliff wall and

Clay Head

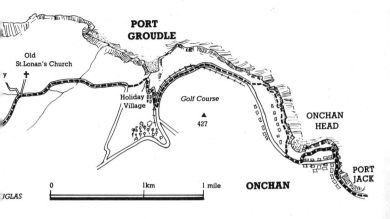

further progress along this line is impossible. At low tide you can walk along the beach but the old path back up to the road has fallen into disuse.

From the promenade a signpost (w/m) indicates a zig-zag path up the hillside to the road where you turn left and soon fork left again on the main road. This is the worst part of the Raad ny Foillan so grit your teeth and follow the busy, pavementless main road for just over a mile.

After crossing the railway and before the road bends right, look for a lane on the left, signpost (w/m). Go down this lane to Garwick Bay, a tiny peaceful haven from the traffic and more like the way of the gull. Cross the stone slab bridge by the boathouse (w/m). As you climb the side of the wooded valley to Baldrine look down to your right across the stream.

There is a maze with a mound of white stones in the centre. The mound of stones aroused some speculation as to its contents. The favoured view was that it is the burial mound of those who could not find the way out!

At the single track road turn left, still uphill, (w/m) and a sign to Clay Head. Keep on this road until the tarmac ends, and the character of the footpath changes yet again.

The sea is far below and distant, the foreground of undulating fields shielding any distant view. About 50yds. along the bridle track is a stile and signpost (w/m), to the right leading into the fields. Cross two fields keeping to the edge and enter a green lane. Turn right at the end of the lane into the next field. Now have faith and follow the instructions carefully!

Celtic cross at Old St. Lonan's Church

Exit from the field through two sheep pens. Before the sheep pen turn left between wooden pallets, (right of way sign), into a narrow hedged path. Escape from this by breathing in and squeezing between the two oil drums. Pass in front of the farmhouse and continue along the lane to join a minor road, signpost (w/m). Turn left and keep on the minor road which leads pleasantly along between blooming hedgerows for 1¼ miles.

A quarter of a mile along this road a track branches off on the left to Old Kirk Lonan. It is but a short distance across the fields and should not be missed by the keen historian.

Old Kirk Lonan or 'the church by the shore' is dedicated to St. Onan, or

Old Kirk Lonan (Old St.Lonan's Church)

Adamnan, an Irish saint who was the Abbot of Iona in 679. The walls to be seen today date back to the 12th century, but the site is much older dating back to the 5th century. In the churchyard in its original position stands a Celtic cross of the 7-9th century. Its decorative bands of plait-work can be clearly seen. Near the church is the old baptismal well, used before the days of the font.

The height gained brings views of the hills to the west as they recede into the distance.

At a right bend keep straight on, using a footpath which soon crosses the railway and descends to cross the stream by Groudle beach.

Leave Port Groudle by the road which winds through the holiday village and turn left when you reach the main road.

The mile along this road is not unpleasant. The traffic has taken the inland road through Onchan and the Raad ny Foillan has only to share it with the odd car and the electric railway. The enjoyment is by no means over. The views keep improving with every step as you round the hill and gain height. To the north Port Groudle and Clay Head appear whilst Douglas to the south heralds journey's end. It was only when I had Douglas spread before me from this vantage point that I realised it took its name from the junction of the River Dhoo with the River Glass.

Robert the Bruce visited the Isle of Man in 1313. He landed at Ramsey

109

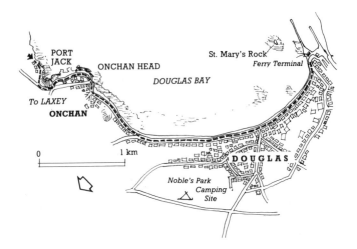

with his army and set off for Castletown, to attack the Scandinavian strong-hold, on the site where Castle Rushen now stands. As you are familiar with the distance, you will appreciate that by the time Bruce and his army had reached Douglas they were very tired and in no fit state to carry on to Castletown, let alone fight a battle. But Douglas was then renowned for its hospitality. Bruce and his army spent the night in the nunnery. They went on to Castletown next day to win the battle and annexe the Island to Scottish rule.

A (w/m) and signpost by the 'Onchan' sign show where to turn left off the road. Go down a narrow footpath with wooden steps which appears to be taking you down the moor and straight off the sheer cliff and into the sea. The path soon levels out and you feel that you are back on the real Raad ny Foillan again. The moor changes to velvet lawns and the footpath into a flagged walk as you progress round Onchan Head. Please treat this section with respect. The right of way is well marked and has been kindly donated by the generous owners to allow you to walk literally through their own back gardens.

On reaching a deep zawn take the footpath left of the garden hedges and keep on this until the path widens and reaches the road again, signpost (w/m). Turn left and left again into King Edward Road which clings to the cliff edge. At the main road keep left along the pavement (w/m) and on to the Douglas promenade. At the southern end of the promenade is the harbour from which we started.

Herring Gull

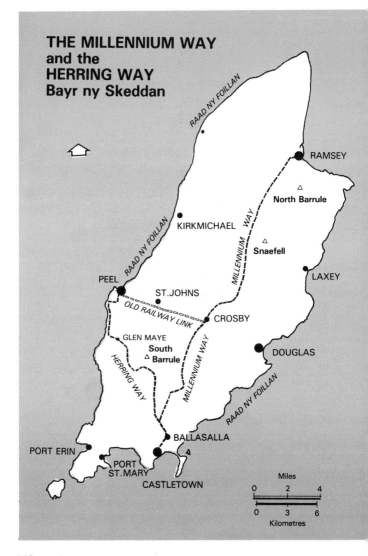

THE MILLENNIUM WAY
and the
HERRING WAY
Bayr ny Skeddan

THE MILLENNIUM WAY

23 miles approximately

Introduction

The Millennium Way was the first long-distance footpath to be established in the Isle of Man. It was timed to coincide with the Millennium year of Tynwald in 1979 and so was named The Millennium Way. It follows as near as possible the ancient route of the kings from Ramsey to Castletown. Ramsey, being on the Sulby river, formed a safe anchorage favoured by the Norse Kings and Castle Rushen, Castletown was the royal residence. The route also passed the ancient site of Tynwald at Keeill Abban.

After a steep climb out of the Sulby valley, open moorland gives fine views out over the northern plain and across the sea to Galloway and the English Lake District. The Way then winds across the western flanks of Snaefell, the cunning line leaving you unaware of the mountain road above, and undisturbed by the civilisation on Snaefell's summit. The infant River Sulby is crossed and a rough ascent to the watershed between Beinn-y-Phott and Carraghan made, yet the ancient pathway re-appears from time to time. An easy descent to the Baldwin valley exchanges the mountain vistas for gentle scented lanes and picturesque rural miniatures.

At Crosby the Way is forced onto the road for 3½ miles. At St. Mark's a traverse of farmland leads west until another short stretch of road drops the Way into the beautiful Silverburn valley. This excellent finish to the walk is shared by the Bayr ny Skeddan. Footpaths by the river lead through Silverburn Glen to Ballasalla and through the fields by the river to Castletown.

The route is well waymarked throughout its length.

It is possible to combine the best parts of the Millennium Way with the Herring Way, by using the footpath along the old railway from Crosby to Peel. This gives a really fine walk through the centre of the island, well worth a special visit.

Interior of the traditional banked wall, exposed on Sky Hill

RAMSEY
to
CROSBY

The Route

The Millennium Way starts just over a mile from Ramsey along the road to Peel. Leave Ramsey by Lezayre Road and if you walk on the right you will soon pass an old milestone informing you that Castletown is 25 miles away.

The land to the north is flat while to the south the slopes of Sky Hill rise almost from the tarmac. The road is following the junction of the sands and gravels with the Barrule Slates of the hills.

Look on the left for the first waymark. It shares a signpost with a finger post pointing to the Mountain Road. A bridle track winds up the wooded hillside of Sky Hill (Skogarfjall meaning wooded hill). In the springtime it is decorated with bluebells, stitchwort, violets and wood sorrel. On leaving the trees behind the path becomes a sheltered sunken way. The bankings are crowned with gorse, high enough to lift the wind, low enough to permit the panorama and as you gain height the panoramas are vast. When you have passed the little spring on the left and come to the Sky Hill boundary gate spend a few minutes enjoying the view.

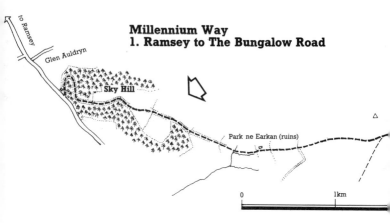

**Millennium Way
1. Ramsey to The Bungalow Road**

To the north-west Jurby church stands white on the coastline. North on a clear day across the sea lies Galloway, Burrow Head and Cairnsmore of Fleet with The Merrick nestling between them on the edge of the horizon. The Point of Ayre Lighthouse can just be seen peeping over the Bride hills and away to the east the mountains of Lakeland, their profiles unfamiliar to those who usually approach them from the M6.

The slopes of Sky Hill that we have just climbed are steeped in Manx history. If the stones of the wall could speak what a tale they would have to tell. Sky Hill was the site of a fierce battle in 1079 when the Norse King Godred Croven attacked the Manx people and defeated them by clever tactics. He set an ambush then advanced with half his men. The Manx attacked from their camp on Sky Hill and 'drove' the Norse king back to the Sulby river. As the Manx army passed the ambush they were caught between the Norsemen and the flooded river where they surrendered. Godred spared them and took over the rule of Man, where he became a respected and much loved king.

The Way now crosses the head of Glentramman and begins to climb gently. North Barrule rises to the south-east and in contrast to the cry of the gull, the serenade of the skylark fills the air.

A three-way signpost clearly indicates the Way is straight on, sharing the public footpath to the Mountain Road. From here you can just make out the cairn on the summit of North Barrule, but you can hardly miss the paraphernalia on the summit of Snaefell. New forestry work on Slieau Managh can be seen to the right and the prominent white quartzy outcrop of Creg Bedn.

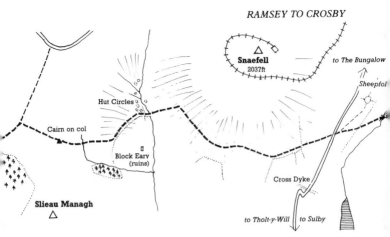

Go through the wicket gate in a stone wall, the forestry fence being on the right. The wall on the left veers off leftwards. Keep straight on to a signpost (w/m), then to a second signpost (w/m) (mind the bog). After the second signpost the Millennium Way turns right along a less distinct track. (The path straight ahead rises steeply to join the Mountain Road.)

Look ahead on the horizon where a cairn can be seen in a slight dip on the ridge, head for it. In about 100yds. a concrete waymark appears and we are back in the old banked pathway heading for the skyline cairn.

As the cairn draws nearer and its neat shape becomes more distinct, you realise that this is no ordinary heap of stones but a cairn of distinction. It was donated by two appreciative travellers and placed in a strategic spot as a key marker on the watershed.

Ahead now is the deep valley of Block Eary. The old track bends right towards the forest and the old farmhouse. Keep straight on crossing a gully and although the path is imaginary there are waymarks to guide you to meet a stone wall. Follow it down to the stream, where there is a stile over the fence and a bridge over the stream.

This is an ideal place for a picnic directly under the summit of Snaefell (2,037ft.). The ancient Manx shepherds must have thought so too, for it was here that they came in summer to pasture their animals. The hummocks of earth on the left as you descended to the stile are shielings, the remains of their summer homes. A better view of them is to be had from across the stream.

117

The Watershed Cairn.

Climb steeply now across the north-west flanks of Snaefell. The path has disappeared but the waymarks and marker poles are frequent. The concrete hexagon markers are set parallel to the path. Look out for one set at right angles. A few yards on the path crosses a small stream and heads right (west) across a slope of rushes. (The waymark pole blends in with the background and may not be immediately apparent.) The Way is now easy to follow as it traverses Snaefell's slopes. A wall rising from the Eary valley climbs nearer then turns away. Continue to traverse as the views to the right over the forests of the Sulby valley unfold and the Sulby reservoir appears. The Way now makes for the wall which it follows until the road is crossed and Snaefell left behind.

The road runs north-west to join the Ramsey-Kirk Michael road near Sulby village and south-east to join the Douglas-Ramsey mountain road at The Bungalow, a halt on the Electric Mountain Railway.

We now have to lose height to cross the infant Sulby river. The path slants down leftwards by a marker pole amongst the rushes. A stile over the wire fence is the next landmark. From here spy out the route ahead up the left-hand bank of the tributary valley.

On the left is a circular sheepfold, best seen from the opposite fell. The workings up the valley are abandoned mines. They proved unproductive and were closed around 1867. An attractive legacy left behind is the pack-horse bridge.

Cross the river by the pack-horse bridge and climb steeply up the left edge of the side valley. When you need a breather turn and admire the sheepfold. I wonder how many hours of toil went into its construction? As you gain the head of the valley the old sunken track re-appears. Slieau Freoghane 1,601ft. and Slieau Dhoo 1,417ft. stand out to the west and Beinn-y-Phott 1,791ft. to the east. An old marker stone of slate is passed on the right and then the mountain road from Brandywell on the Douglas-Ramsey road to Kirk Michael is crossed.

The going is easy now. The track is locked between moorland embankments and as the watershed is reached, Carraghan 1,640ft. rises directly in front of you.

At the next junction keep left (w/m) on the bridle track. The southern half of the Island is spread out before you as the track descends through five gates to a plantation becoming more stony as you descend.

The track (Raad Garroo - rough road) runs down the ridge between the West Baldwin and the East Baldwin valleys. The West Baldwin valley is

Looking back to Snaefell from the slopes of Beinn y Phott.
Note the circular sheepfold.

Millennium Way
2. The Bungalow Road to Baldwin

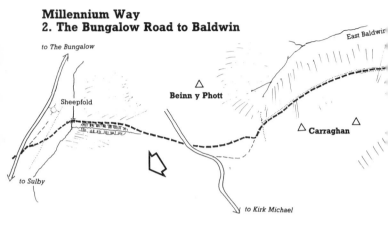

lined with forest. Streams tumble noisily into the reservoir and a quiet road
creeps along the water's edge and climbs up the wooded slopes to the head of
the valley. If you wish to sample its delights turn right at the intake wall,
cross the moor then follow the edge of the plantation into the valley.

The miners' packhorse bridge over the infant Sulby river

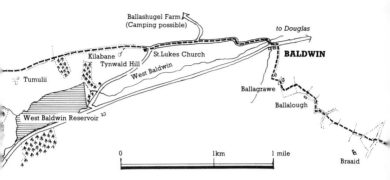

Continue down the track and as soon as St. Luke's chapel comes into view look for an old, yet prominent stone stile on the right.

Just over the stile is Cronk Keeill Abban, one of the three Tynwald mounds in the Island. The first primitive Tynwald was described in the Sagas. The chieftain chose a mound then erected an altar to Thor. He then made a fence of tree trunks or planted trees leading to the mound. After the prayers and ceremony the chieftain would sit and listen to the woes of his subjects, pronounce his decisions and the new laws. It was here that the decision to settle quarrels by court and not by feud was initiated. The next site of interest is St. Luke's Chapel-of-Ease. The present chapel was built

St. Luke's Chapel-of-Ease.   121

The West Baldwin valley

in 1836 on the site of the ancient Celtic church, Keeill Abban. A plaque of red sandstone is built into the gable below the bell, an ancient carved stone like a little garnet in its country rock.

Beyond the chapel we join the road and bear left walking gently downhill. Go straight on at the road junction (w/m) and descend to the Baldwin valley.

You will have to scout around for the next waymark. It is across two bridges and is hidden at the foot of the second lane on the right.

A stony lane leads steeply up the valley side through a haze of colour: celandine, bluebells, primroses and the delicate yellow poppy in a springtime backcloth of ransoms and honeysuckle.

The lane bends to the left, revealing a fine view of the hills and St. Luke's chapel in its setting. At the end of the lane pass in front of the cottage to a stile on the right. Look for the signpost (Millennium Way and Public Footpath) to guide you through a gate and diagonally across the field. The Way now is across the front of the farm to the right. The waymark stands in a background of trees and is not readily distinguished from this point. Past the farm continue along the field edge until you can go through a little green gate and stone stile by a stand of trees into a lane. Along the lane you will come to a three-way junction where we take to the fields again over a high ladder stile (w/m).

122

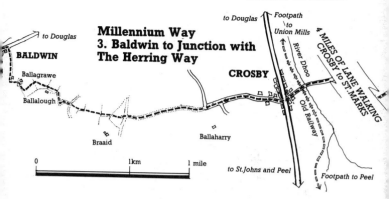

Cross two fields. The exit to the second is on the far right over a stile hidden by, but not overgrown with gorse. The next waymark is best seen from the top of that stile where you can plan a direct line across the field. It held a fine crop of hay when I was there. Try to maintain a single track and keep the path width to a minimum.

We are now back on a lane. Turn left down the lane to join a tarmac road (w/m) which leads downhill into the Neb valley and Crosby.

CROSBY
Accommodation
B&B
Camping - Baldwin - Balshugel Farm. Tel: Marown 851235

Public Transport
Bus Douglas-Peel

Services
Post office, general store, toilets, garage.

123

St. Patrick's Chair.

CROSBY
to
CASTLETOWN

Cross straight over the main road and past the park to the old railway and the river bridge.

The old railway is now a public footpath to Peel along the pretty Neb valley, passing through St. John's village and close by Tynwald Hill. It joins the Bayr ny Skeddan at Glenfaba bridge half a mile from Peel. This route is highly recommended to link the two walks into one.

The Millennium Way now continues along the road for 3½ miles. At the top of the hill is Marown School, 1874, a church school of the days when children began when 5 years old and stayed at the same school throughout their school life.

The next site of interest is just beyond the road junction. Keep straight across and the church on the right is St. Runan's.

There has been a Keeill on this site since the 7th century. Ronan or Marown was a Scottish saint indicating missionaries to the Island from Scotland.

Another half a mile on the road will bring you to a bridle track on the right leading to St. Patick's Chair, signpost. A few minutes walk up the track brings you to a stile in the hedge on the left. St. Patrick's Chair is in the centre of the field.

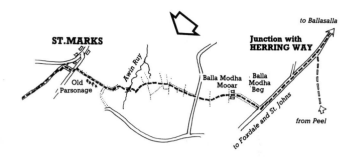

This is a group of standing stones, two of them carved with crosses. It is told that St. Patrick preached from this spot and anyone who sits to rest with his back against one of the carved stones will never feel fatigued again.

The road continues to climb passing Slieau Chiarn 636ft. on your left. As you reach the crest Castletown comes into view across the southern plain. Cross the Douglas-Foxdale road and pass by Ballacallin Mooar and Ballanicholas. We now descend to cross the Santon Burn.

Granite boulders left behind by the Ice Age glaciers were washed down by the stream and can still be seen in the river bed. Many of these boulders have been removed and incorporated into local buildings.

Cross Campbell's bridge with its interesting inscription and carry straight on at the next road junction where the Foxdale road goes off right. A mile further on is the village of St. Mark's.

At a road junction turn right, then go left, cross over the road and turn right at the waymark. The lane leading past the old parsonage is lined with a variety of overgrown shrubs and is well used. It soon swings away to the right and we go straight ahead through a gate (Public Footpath sign) where it quickly deteriorates into a waterlogged and muddy track. At the three-way signpost the Way carries straight on towards Ballamodha road. Pause awhile at the red gate on the left and look ahead for two white signposts on the opposite hillside to indicate your intended direction. The lane bends to a gate and stile (w/m). Cross the field and turn left along the side of the brook which you cross by an old stone slab bridge and continue on the right-hand bank until you turn right over a stile (w/m). Cross diagonally left to the top corner of the field (w/m) into a green lane. The green lane is short and the next waymark turns you right to a kissing gate in the far hedge. Go straight on across the next three fields. Cross the lane and

125

Barn with granite boulders, at Ballamodha Beg

the following field (w/m's) into an enclosed lane leading into the Balla-modha Mooar farmyard. Cross the yard into the farm lane. As you pass the next farm, Ballamodha Beg, notice the use of the granite boulders and slate in the construction of the farm buildings.

At the road turn left to meet the Bayr ny Skeddan at the Silverburn bridge.

The walk from Silverburn to Castletown is described in the Bayr ny Skeddan (see page 136).

BAYR NY SKEDDAN

HERITAGE YEAR 1986

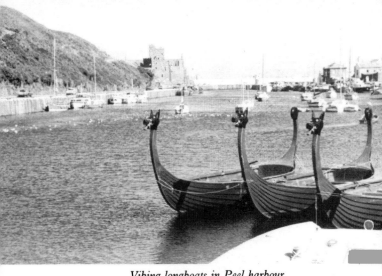

Viking longboats in Peel harbour

BAYR NY SKEDDAN
The Herring Way

14 miles approximately

The Bayr ny Skeddan as may be expected begins by the kipper factory in Peel. It follows the River Neb upstream to Glenfaba from where it climbs the slopes of Corrin's Hill to join the Raad ny Foillan. The coastline is then followed south for 1½ miles allowing you to enjoy the vast seascapes and admire the skill of the sea birds as they ride the updraught from the plunging cliffs. The descent into Glen Maye brings a complete contrast. The picturesque Glen is followed, first through a narrow verdant valley, then passing through forests to finally open out onto the high moorland between Cronk ny Arrey Laa and South Barrule to the watershed at The Round Table.

The Way then crosses the slopes of South Barrule high above the Cringle Reservoir to descend interestingly along old lanes and by farm paths to meet the St. Johns - Castletown road, the Millennium Way and the Silverburn valley. A riverside path now leads through Silverdale Glen to Ballasalla and Rushen Abbey. Continuing to follow the Silverburn, the flat coastal plain presents an unusual view of Castletown until the Way ends as the river enters the harbour at the castle gates.

The old mill wheel, Glenfaba.

The Route

Start at the harbour bridge by a huge old anchor, attractively displayed but of unknown origin.

The fishing boats are rather strangely named. Cornishmen came to fish for herring in 1850. Their boats had a different rig to the Manx boats. Most of the Cornishmen were named Nicholas and their boats became known as 'Nickeys'. As the Manx fishermen modernised their boats in the Cornish style, they too kept the name 'Nickeys'. (p. 135)

The waymark is by the Kipper Factory fence on a signpost 'Public Footpath to Glenfaba'. Take the gruesome track between the factories, put your fingers in your ears to block the noise of the power station, hold your handerchief over your nose to escape the exhaust of its huge diesel engines and sprint the first hundred yards of the Bayr ny Skeddan.

The path takes the old railway by the River Neb.

The old mill leat is still active, bringing water to cool the power station's diesel generators. At the old disused mill across the river a small water-wheel can be seen.

The path leads under a bridge. This is Glenfaba. Just beyond the bridge is a fine pair of water-wheels worth seeing, with the leat and sluices still in place. A path and steps to the right lead up onto the road

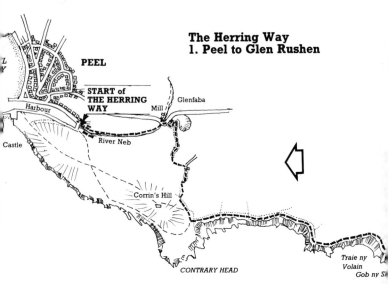

The Herring Way
1. Peel to Glen Rushen

bridge. Cross the river and the road, then take the lane right by the side of a cottage (w/m). The lane now winds uphill leaving the Neb valley behind, and in front the Corrin's Hill looks impressive. Where the lane forks keep straight uphill. The lane is now between high banks and the nettles, flowers and trickle of water attract butterflies making the climb pass quickly. As the lane bends keep left, then right, until at its end you can cross a stile on the right to the open fell on Corrin's Hill.

A panorama of mountains lies inland. To the north of St. John's lie Beary Mountain 1,020ft., Coldon 1,599ft., Carraghan 1,640ft. In the far background is Snaefell 2,036ft. framed against Sartfell 1,490ft., and Slieau Freoghane 1,610ft. To the south of St. John's stands Slieau Whillain, 1,094ft. or the Witches' Hill.

Tradition tells that those suspected of witchcraft were taken to the top of the hill and placed in a barrel into which iron spikes had been driven. The barrel was then rolled down the hill. If the unfortunate victim was found to be dead at the bottom then she had received her just deserts. However, if she was still alive she was obviously a witch and was burnt at the stake.

Turn left by the wall and as the path levels out a beautiful scene appears.

130

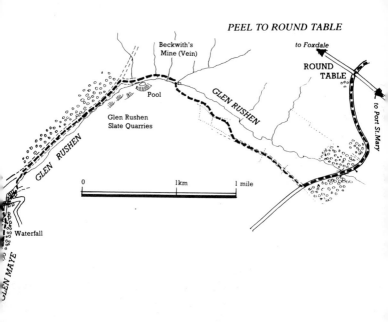

The coastline hills, their foundations touched by the sea, stand looking west. Cronk ny Arree Laa, Lhiattee ny Beinnee and Bradda Hill with the tail of Niarbyl pointing a challenge at the waves.

At the wicket gate we join the Raad ny Foillan for a few miles. Go through the gate (w/m) and follow the coastal path south.

This is a magnificent path, high above the sea. After crossing the field wall by a stile, skirting a spring, and returning to the cliff top, the next headland, Gob ny Sharray, has a wide grassy crown.

Here is the place to see the colonies of nesting herring gulls and fulmar and to make friends with the stonechat. I couldn't help smiling at its call, a shrill 'peep' then 'grunt, grunt' like a primadonna clearing her throat. In spring the path is clothed with primroses and white campion. Bluebells grow with stunted stems and huge crowded flowers of dark purple.

The path descends into Glen Maye. Here we part from the Raad ny Foillan and turn inland (w/m). The official route turns left up the narrow road but a better alternative is to leave the Way here to walk up the Glen footpath. Cross the road and enter the gate by the site of the Mona Erin water-wheel. A plaque on the wall tells you its history. As you progress up the Glen you will appreciate that it is a place of rare

131

The waterfall, Glen Maye

beauty. Take the Waterfall Path and take your time to absorb the ferns and plants in their lovely setting. A path branches left for people to admire the waterfall, then climbs steeply to cross a bridge over the stream and emerge from the gorge to meet the narrow road at the local café, hotel, gift shop and toilets.

Cross the main road and turn right. Cross the river bridge and branch left down a small lane. No waymark. Turn left again down a path at the Public Footpath sign to Glen Rushen. Keep right to gain the river bank. Cross the river and carry on upstream to join a redundant minor road which is closed to traffic and the tarmac is fighting a losing battle with the grass.

Across the now deepening valley the hillside is covered with cobwebs of bluebells. Clear streams tumble through the forest as you progress up the valley. Old slate quarry workings with their spoil heaps can be seen high on the opposite hillside.

Pass through the forest and fork right at the junction (w/m). An old dam on the right with a strange wire canopy is part of the Peel water supply.

Notice how the river colour changes. The River Maye (maye is Manx for yellow) has suddenly begun to live up to its name. On the hillside above

132

Glen Rushen. In the background are old mine buildings at
Beckwith's Vein

was one of the principal lead mines of the Island. The Foxdale vein ran for three miles in an east-west direction. Of the thirteen shafts sunk, Beckwith's lies just above this 'yellow outlet'. It was a chance discovery. A man driving his haycart noticed a mass of lead ore (galena) in the heather. The ore contained a considerable amount of silver and was worked until 1910. Beckwith's shaft reaches a depth of 1,100ft. which is 500ft. below sea level. The mine was closed when prices fell and the operation became uneconomic, but it is not worked out and to date licences are still held. The spoil heaps and full extent of the workings can be seen as we progress up Glen Rushen.

Cross the river by the named bridge and keep to the right of the water supply catchment area. A stile and (w/m) direct you onto a small path running steeply up the hillside to the next (w/m) where you can turn for a view of the mines and the slopes of South Barrule. The next stile enters the Forestry Department, Creg ny Crock. The path climbs steadily to the next waymark by an old ruined farmhouse. Turn left along the forest track. On the left is a small wooden shelter. If you use it, please take your litter away and close the door. The track now crosses a few small streams as it passes through the new plantation.

**The Herring Way
2. Round Table to Ballasalla**

The seedlings in the new plantation nestle in the furrows unlike the English plantations where they are planted on the ridges. This is to protect them from the wind and to give access to any moisture available in the usually dry spring weather on the western side of the Island. The track to the road has been newly laid and forms a tapestry underfoot. The silken texture of the mica-laden slate is especially appreciated if glinting in half sunlight, its grey forming a subtle blend with the orange streaks of iron and the white of the quartz.

Turn left at the main road (w/m), cross over the bridge and with South Barrule on the left, Cronk ny Arree Laa on the right, keep straight on to gain the crossroads at Round Table quickly and easily.

Cross the Port Erin-Foxdale road (w/m).

The views from here are extensive in all directions as you come over the watershed. From Glen Maye we have climbed steadily to 1,000ft. above sea level and from now on it is downhill all the way.

Turn left at the corner of the Cringle Plantation onto a stony track by the forest side. The track mounts a slight brow where a new forestry road branches right. Keep straight on. Another track joins from the right. Here we can see some quartz boulders built into the wall.

Keep straight on down the hill with the Silverburn valley and the Cringle Reservoir on the right. At the crossroads turn left (w/m) along the road until you meet a right turn to Ballamodha Farm and

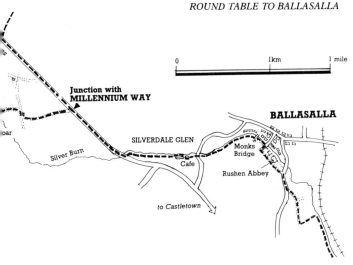

Glenmoar Farm (w/m). The farm lane descends by a little stream until it flows into a busy duckpond at Old Moaney. Turn right (waymark on the barn side), then left into an enclosed lane through a gate. Keep straight on and follow the right-hand edge of the field to a stile, Public Footpath sign. Turn left along the old embanked lane and straight on through the farmyard at Moaney Mooar, where the lane becomes wider and smoother. The lane bends right then left before it joins the main road. Turn right down the hill past an old milestone to the Silverburn Bridge.

In Silverdale

JUNCTION with the
MILLENNIUM WAY

The Bayr ny Skeddan has now joined the Millennium Way. What a meeting place of travellers this must have been, what a place of gossip for friends from the north and the west and a welcome rest for the pack-animals while tales were told. A place of goodbyes and well-wishes for those returning home.

Cross the Silverburn Bridge and turn left onto the riverbank path (w/m). Cross the leat and walk between the leat and the burn through the shady woodland. Suddenly you realise that the turf is mown and the rushing leat has emptied its water into a small lake. This is Silverburn Glen. The footpath goes straight ahead past the lake.

There is a café in the old mill building and the water-wheel is in working order but I enjoyed watching the tiny water-wheel. Its power has been harnessed to drive a carousel which revolves at a gentle pace to the sound of the falling water.

The Monks Bridge, Ballasalla

Exit at the glen car park by the road and regain the riverside woodland at the waymark on the left. The footpath passes a gate at the glen entrance and you will notice from looking at the river bed that you are now in an area of limestone. The limestone steps of the next stile are very polished and slippery when wet.

The Monks' Bridge over the Silverburn was built by the monks of Rushen Abbey in 1350. It is a picturesque double-arched bridge paved with quartz cobbles.

Do not cross the Monks' Bridge but go straight on. At the ford the footbridge is the nearest way to the centre of Ballasalla and the shops. From the ford the footpath makes its way around the right-hand side of Rushen Abbey. If you want to visit the ruins keep straight on.

Rushen Abbey, although small, played an important part in Manx history. In 1134 Olaf I gave permission to the Abbot of Furness Abbey to build an abbey in Ballasalla. In 1147 it came under the rule of the Cistercian Order. The monks were farmers and lived on the results of their work. They became known as experts in land drainage and eventually the Abbot had under his influence the best farmland, the mining and also the fishing. The Abbot of Rushen was a baron in his own right and owned two sets of gallows where he exercised judgement over life and death. Today only a few ruins remain although the good Norman arch of the north transept is still intact.

The Herring Way
3. Ballasalla to Castletown

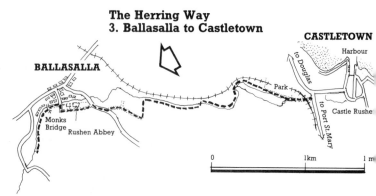

Beyond the Abbey cross the main road and a short way up the hill the Bayr ny Skeddan/Millennium Way branches left. Keep straight on at the wicket gate and along the track. Turn left down a grassy path to an old ruined barn by the river (w/m). Turn right along the riverside. Just across the water is the railway and if a train goes by you will have a grandstand view of the gleaming engine. The path runs along the bank of the river until it crosses to the left bank at a bridge. Here you will have the same view of Castle Rushen as the fishermen from Peel must have looked for with anticipation. Keep straight along the path past the park. Cross the road and in a few minutes you will reach journey's end at Castletown Harbour.

The path follows the Silver Burn to Castletown

Castle Rushen, Castletown

GLOSSARY OF MANX WORDS

Sc - Scandinavian origin   *C* - Celtic origin

Agneash (SC) Edge, nose

Andreas Andrew

Ayre (Sc) A pebbly beach

Balla (C) Farm or homestead

Barrule (Sc) Warool = Wardfell of ward and watch

Bradda (Sc) Broad headland

Cass-ny-Hawin (C) The end of the river

Cornaa (Sc) Water-wheel

*Cronk (C)*Hill

Cregneish/Creagneish (Sc) Craukness - the ness of the crows

Dhoon (C) Fort

Douglas (C) The dark stream

Ellan Vannin Isle of Man

Fleshwick (Sc) Fles-vik green creek

Gog (C) Mouth

Jurby (Sc) Ingvar-byr - Invar's home

Laxey (Sc) Salmon river

Langness (Sc) Long headland

Lhen (C) A trench

Maye - Glen (C) The yellow glen

Meayll or Mull (C) Maol, bare

Mooar Glen (C) The great glen

Niarbyl (C) Yn arby, the tail

Peel (Sc) A fortress

Poyllvaaish (C) Pool of death

Purt/Phurt Harbour, port

Ramsey (Sc) Island of garlic

Ronaldsway (C) Ronald's boat path

Rue (C) Red point

Santon Santon - St. Sanctain

Scarlett Skarfakluft - cormorants ledge

Slieau (C) Mountain

Soderick (Sc) Sol-vik - sunny creek

Sumark Primrose

Wyllin (Glen) (C) The mill glen

BIBLIOGRAPHY

Airne C.W.   *The Story of the Isle of Man* Vol I & II 1964.

Allan D.E.   *The Flowering Plants of the Isle of Man.*

Caine W.Ralph Hall   *The Isle of Man.* 1909.

Corrin H.S.   *The Isle of Man.* 1977.

Crockett S.R.   *The Raiders.* 1954.

Cullen J.P. & Jennings P.P.   *Birds of the Isle of Man.* 1986.

Falconar A.E.I.   *Celtic Tales of Myth and Fantasy.* 1984.

Herbert Agnes   *The Isle of Man.* 1909.

Lockington Marshall W.   *The Calf of Man.* 1978.

Memoirs   *Geological Survey of Great Britain.* 1954.

Moseley   *The Geology of the Lake District.* 1978.

Palmer T.   *Discover the Isle of Man.* 1987.

Stenning E.H.   *The County Books - The Isle of Man.* 1950.

Stenning E.H.   *Portrait of the Isle of Man.* 1983.

Whittaker's Almanac. 1987.

Fuchsia

CICERONE GUIDES

Cicerone publish a wide range of reliable guides to walking and climbing in Britain - and other general interest books

LAKE DISTRICT - General Books
LAKELAND VILLAGES
WORDSWORTH'S DUDDON REVISITED
THE REGATTA MEN
REFLECTIONS ON THE LAKES
OUR CUMBRIA
PETTIE
THE HIGH FELLS OF LAKELAND
CONISTON COPPER A History
LAKELAND - A taste to remember (Recipes)
THE LOST RESORT?
CHRONICLES OF MILNTHORPE
LOST LANCASHIRE

LAKE DISTRICT - Guide Books
CASTLES IN CUMBRIA
WESTMORLAND HERITAGE WALK
IN SEARCH OF WESTMORLAND
CONISTON COPPER MINES
SCRAMBLES IN THE LAKE DISTRICT
MORE SCRAMBLES IN THE LAKE DISTRICT
WINTER CLIMBS IN THE LAKE DISTRICT
WALKS IN SILVERDALE/ARNSIDE
BIRDS OF MORECAMBE BAY
THE EDEN WAY

NORTHERN ENGLAND (outside the Lakes
THE YORKSHIRE DALES A walker's guide
WALKING IN THE SOUTH PENNINES
LAUGHS ALONG THE PENNINE WAY
WALKS IN THE YORKSHIRE DALES (3 VOL)
WALKS TO YORKSHIRE WATERFALLS
NORTH YORK MOORS Walks
THE CLEVELAND WAY & MISSING LINK
DOUGLAS VALLEY WAY
THE RIBBLE WAY
WALKING NORTHERN RAILWAYS EAST
WALKING NORTHERN RAILWAYS WEST
HERITAGE TRAILS IN NW ENGLAND
BIRDWATCHING ON MERSEYSIDE
THE LANCASTER CANAL
FIELD EXCURSIONS IN NW ENGLAND
ROCK CLIMBS LANCASHIRE & NW
THE ISLE OF MAN COASTAL PATH

DERBYSHIRE & EAST MIDLANDS
WHITE PEAK WALKS - 2 Vols
HIGH PEAK WALKS
WHITE PEAK WAY
KINDER LOG
THE VIKING WAY
THE DEVIL'S MILL (Novel)
WHISTLING CLOUGH (Novel)
WALES & WEST MIDLANDS
THE RIDGES OF SNOWDONIA
HILLWALKING IN SNOWDONIA
ASCENT OF SNOWDON
WELSH WINTER CLIMBS
SNOWDONIA WHITE WATER SEA & SURF
SCRAMBLES IN SNOWDONIA
ROCK CLIMBS IN WEST MIDLANDS
THE SHROPSHIRE HILLS A Walker's Guide

SOUTH & SOUTH WEST ENGLAND
WALKS IN KENT
THE WEALDWAY & VANGUARD WAY
SOUTH DOWNS WAY & DOWNS LINK
COTSWOLD WAY
WALKING ON DARTMOOR
SOUTH WEST WAY - 2 Vol

SCOTLAND
SCRAMBLES IN LOCHABER
SCRAMBLES IN SKYE
THE ISLAND OF RHUM
CAIRNGORMS WINTER CLIMBS
WINTER CLIMBS BEN NEVIS & GLENCOE
SCOTTISH RAILWAY WALKS
TORRIDON A Walker's Guide
SKI TOURING IN SCOTLAND

THE MOUNTAINS OF ENGLAND & WALES
VOL 1 WALES
VOL 2 ENGLAND

Also a full range of guidebooks to walking, scrambling, ice-climbing, rock climbing, and other adventurous pursuits in Europe

Other guides are constantly being added to the Cicerone List.
Available from bookshops, outdoor equipment shops or direct (send for price list)
from CICERONE, 2 POLICE SQUARE, MILNTHORPE, CUMBRIA, LA7 7PY

CICERONE GUIDES

Cicerone publish a wide range of reliable guides to walking and climbing in Europe

FRANCE
TOUR OF MONT BLANC
CHAMONIX MONT BLANC - A Walking Guide
TOUR OF THE OISANS: GR54
WALKING THE FRENCH ALPS: GR5
THE CORSICAN HIGH LEVEL ROUTE: GR20
THE WAY OF ST JAMES: GR65
THE PYRENEAN TRAIL: GR10
TOUR OF THE QUEYRAS
ROCK CLIMBS IN THE VERDON

FRANCE / SPAIN
WALKS AND CLIMBS IN THE PYRENEES
ROCK CLIMBS IN THE PYRENEES

SPAIN
WALKS & CLIMBS IN THE PICOS DE EUROPA
WALKING IN MALLORCA
BIRDWATCHING IN MALLORCA
COSTA BLANCA CLIMBS

FRANCE / SWITZERLAND
THE JURA - Walking the High Route and
  Winter Ski Traverses
CHAMONIX TO ZERMATT The Walker's Haute
Route

SWITZERLAND
WALKS IN THE ENGADINE
THE VALAIS - A Walking Guide
THE ALPINE PASS ROUTE

GERMANY / AUSTRIA
THE KALKALPEN TRAVERSE
KLETTERSTEIG - Scrambles
WALKING IN THE BLACK FOREST
MOUNTAIN WALKING IN AUSTRIA
WALKING IN THE SALZKAMMERGUT
KING LUDWIG WAY

ITALY
ALTA VIA - High Level Walkis in the Dolomites
VIA FERRATA - Scrambles in the Dolomites
ITALIAN ROCK - Selected Rock Climbs in
  Northern Italy
CLASSIC CLIMBS IN THE DOLOMITES
WALKING IN THE DOLOMITES

OTHER AREAS
THE MOUNTAINS OF GREECE - A Walker's
Guide
CRETE: Off the beaten track
Treks & Climbs in the mountains of RHUM &
PETRA, JORDAN
THE ATLAS MOUNTAINS

GENERAL OUTDOOR BOOKS
LANDSCAPE PHOTOGRAPHY
FIRST AID FOR HILLWALKERS
MOUNTAIN WEATHER
MOUNTAINEERING LITERATURE
THE ADVENTURE ALTERNATIVE

CANOEING
SNOWDONIA WILD WATER, SEA & SURF
WILDWATER CANOEING
CANOEIST'S GUIDE TO THE NORTH EAST

CARTOON BOOKS
ON FOOT & FINGER
ON MORE FEET & FINGERS
LAUGHS ALONG THE PENNINE WAY

 CICERONE

*Also a full range of guidebooks
to walking, scrambling, ice-climbing,
rock climbing, and other adventurous
pursuits in Britain and abroad*

---

*Other guides are constantly being added to the Cicerone List.
Available from bookshops, outdoor equipment shops or direct (send for price list)
from CICERONE, 2 POLICE SQUARE, MILNTHORPE, CUMBRIA, LA7 7PY*